25 WAL

In and Ar

ABERDEEN

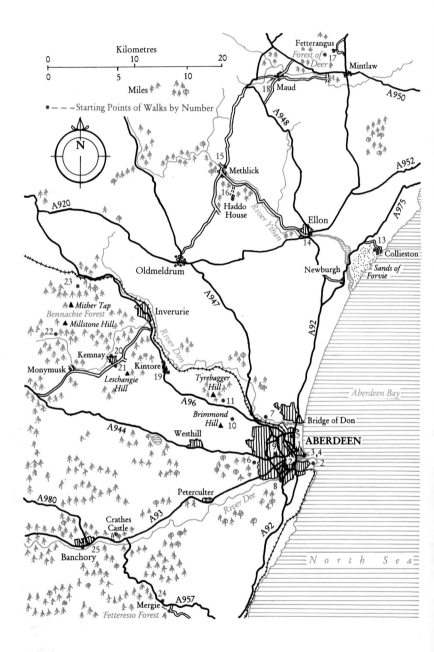

Kilometres
0   10   20

Miles
0   5   10

●— — —Starting Points of Walks by Number

N

Fetterangus
Forest of Deer   17
Mintlaw
A950
18 Maud
A948
A952
15 Methlick
A920
16   River Ythan
Haddo House
Ellon
14
13 Collieston
Oldmeldrum
Newburgh   Sands of Forvie
A975
23
▲ Mither Tap
Bennachie Forest
▲ Millstone Hill
Inverurie
A947
22
River Don
Kemnay   20
Monymusk   21 Kintore
Leschangie Hill   19
Tyrebagger Hill
▲ 11
A96
Brimmond Hill▲ 10
A944
Westhill
Aberdeen Bay
7
Bridge of Don
ABERDEEN
3, 4
6   2   2
8
Peterculter
River Dee
A980
A93
Crathes Castle
A92
25
Banchory
North Sea
24
Mergie   A957
Fetteresso Forest

25 WALKS

In and Around

ABERDEEN

Robert Smith

Series Editor: Roger Smith

GrampianHighlands&Aberdeen

EDINBURGH:HMSO

Applications for reproduction should be made to HMSO

Acknowledgements

The publishers thanks are due to Grampian, Highlands and Aberdeen, Tourism and Marketing Company and the author Robert Smith, for access to and use of transparencies throughout the book.

British Library Cataloguing in Publication Data

A catalogue record for this book is available from the British Library

Cover Illustration: The Salvation Army Citadel in the Castlegate . . . the start of the walk along Union Street, known to generations of Aberdonians as the Mat. Silhouetted in the forground is the Mannie o' the Well, a familiar statue topping a well on the Plainstones. The old Mercat Cross can be seen in front (left) of the Citadel. Picture by Robert Smith

ISBN 0 11 495261 2

CONTENTS

USEFUL INFORMATION

The length of each walk is given in kilometres and miles, but within the text measurements are metric for simplicity. The walks are described in detail and are supported by accompanying maps (study them before you start the walk), so there is little likelihood of getting lost, but if you want a back-up you will find the 1:25 000 Pathfinder Ordnance Survey maps on sale locally.

Every care has been taken to make the descriptions and maps as accurate as possible, but the author and publishers can accept no responsibility for errors, however caused. The countryside is always changing and there will inevitably be alterations to some aspects of these walks as time goes by. The publishers and author would be happy to receive comments and suggested alterations for future editions of the book.

In the text the word 'path' is used for a purely pedestrian route, 'track' for private, unsurfaced but motorable routes (such as farm and forestry tracks) and 'road' for a tarred, public way.

A reminder about country behaviour: farm gates must be closed when used, farm buildings and machinery left alone, dogs kept on leads near livestock, growing crops avoided, matches not tossed aside or litter dropped. Routes described may or may not be rights-of-way. Farmers are usually friendly folk who work long hours to maintain the land we enjoy. When you meet, be helpful and friendly too!

METRIC MEASUREMENTS

At the beginning of each walk, the distance is given in miles and kilometres. Within the text, all measurements are metric for simplicity (and indeed our Ordnance Survey maps are now all metric). However, it was felt that a conversion table might be useful to those readers who, like the author, still tend to think in Imperial terms.

The basic statistic to remember is that one kilometre is five-eighths of a mile. Half a mile is equivalent to 800 metres and a quarter-mile is 400 metres. Below that distance, yards and metres are little different in practical terms.

km	miles
1	0.625
1.6	1
2	1.25
3	1.875
3.2	2
4	2.5
4.8	3
5	3.125
6	3.75
6.4	4
7	4.375
8	5
9	5.625
10	6.25
16	10

INTRODUCTION

Aberdeen was once described by the poet Iain Crichton Smith as a "town of pure crystal". He loved its "brilliant streets" and the sight of mica glittering on its white stone. It is a city of ganite and roses – it won so many Britain in Bloom competitions that it was debarred from taking part in the contest.

This, then, is the setting for *In and Around Aberdeen,* which takes you on 25 walks in the Granite City and in the countryside around it. It is a book for visitors *and* Aberdonians, for local folk will find that it throws new light on familiar scenes.

You can start by Walking the Mat. The Mat is Aberdeen's main street, Union Street, where "boy met girl" when generations of youngsters once strolled there on a Sunday evening. Now you can learn more about what was called "the finest street in the Empire." Explore, too, the city's exclusive West End, where magnificent buildings show Rubislaw granite at its best.

Aberdeen has been called the Silver City with the Golden Sands, so the book takes you to the seaside to walk the Prom, to wander round the Bay of Nigg to Girdleness Lighthouse and the old Torry Battery, and to visit the busy harbour, where huge oil vessels have taken the place of the port's disappearing trawler fleet.

Then you can take a trip up the old Deeside railway line – on foot. This walk follows the route of the old "Subbie" trains and passes through some lovely Royal Deeside scenery. There is another kind of charm in Old Aberdeen – the Aulton – with King's College and its chapel, the old Town House, St Machar's Cathedral and a path above the River Don that takes you to the historic Brig o' Balgownie.

These are some of the walks in Aberdeen, but there are others beyond the city boundary. All are within easy reach of the city. For those without cars, details are given of bus services available. They range from Deeside to Donside, into Buchan, south to the Mearns, and along the North-east coast to the Sands of Forvie.

You'll find plenty of variety . . . crossing the Braes o' Gight to the ruins of brooding Gight Castle, walking in the stately grounds of Haddo Country Park, visiting historic Crathes Castle, climbing an Observatory overlooking an abandoned racecourse, or strolling by an old Aberdeenshire canal. That's a taste of what lies in store for you – there is much more.

The walks range from 5 km (3 miles) to 11 km (7 miles) and are ideal for the family. There are detailed maps to help you. Advice on what to wear, the terrain, toilets and transport, refreshments and opening hours can be found in the Information panels. Whether walking in what has been called the "granite grandery" of Aberdeen, or in the countryside, this book will help to make it a rich and rewarding experience.

ROBERT SMITH

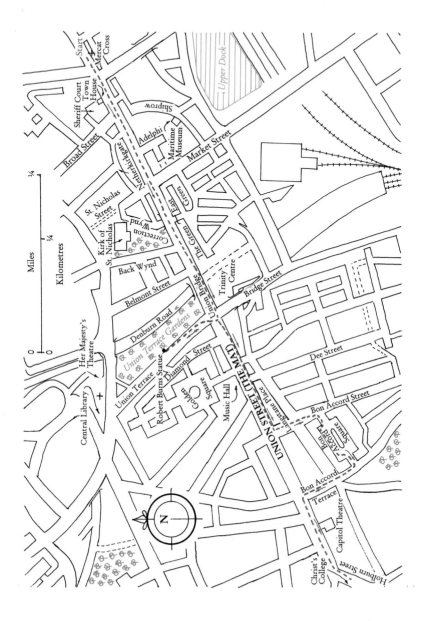

THE MAT

Walking the Mat is an old Aberdeen custom. The Mat is the city's main street, Union Street, where generations of youngsters once strolled on a Sunday evening. Here, boy met girl and romance blossomed under the flickering lamplight of what was said to be "the finest street in the Empire".

Aberdonians claim that Union Street, which celebrated its 200th anniversary in 1994, is still the finest street in the world. They will also tell you that it hasn't lost any of its romance, although Walking the Mat has almost become a thing of the past.

The street is to Aberdeen what the Royal Mile is to Edinburgh. It is also a mile in length, but at one time it was measured by the phrase "fae the Duke tae Babbie Law". Babbie Law was a shopkeeper at Holburn Junction and the Duke was George, 5th Duke of Gordon, whose statue once stood in the Castlegate. It is here, in the historic heart of the city, that we begin to Walk the Mat.

If the Duke is no longer there to send you on your way, the Mannie o' the Well will see you off. The Mannie is a three-and-a-half feet (1 m) high statue topping a well in the Castlegate, near the old Mercat Cross. It stood in Castle Street until 1852, when its removal to the Green caused an uproar.

The Mannie was finally moved back to the Castlegate and now stands on the restored Plainstones near the Union Buildings, which contain the Royal Athenaeum. This granite block was designed by the city's famous architect, Archibald Simpson. The work of Simpson and John Smith (Tudor Johnnie, the city's first official architect), can be seen all along Union Street.

Beyond the Union Buildings, the Shiprow, where city shipmasters and Provosts once lived, sweeps down to the harbour. The home of Provost John Ross

INFORMATION

Distance: 3 km (2 miles)

Start and finish: Castlegate. Multi-storey car park in Shiprow, also car parks in East North Street and Gallowgate.

Terrain: Pavements. No special footwear needed.

Public transport: Continuous bus services on Union Street. Information and timetables from Grampian Transport, 395 King Street, Aberdeen (Tel: 01224 637047), also from Tourist Information Centre, Broad Street, Aberdeen (Tel: 01224 632727).

Toilets: Main public toilets for Union Street are at Union Terrace Gardens. Also at Bon Accord Centre and at Music Hall.

Opening hours: *Aberdeen Maritime Museum*, Shiprow, Mon.-Sat. 1000–1700. *St Nicholas Church and kirkyard*, and *Union Terrace Gardens*, are also worth seeing.

Town House through Market Cross arches.

(1710–11) now houses the Aberdeen Maritime Museum. Looking across Union Street from the top of the Shiprow you can see the Sheriff Court buildings and the Town House.

The building of the city's main thoroughfare meant cutting through the north shoulder of St Catherine's Hill, whose highest point is where the Adelphi is today. The arched entrance to Adelphi Court, as it was originally called, is on your left as you head up Union Street. It is gradually being restored to its former glory.

Further on is Market Street, the main route to the Harbour and Torry, while on the right is St Nicholas Street – or what is left of it. Not so many years ago the old "trammies" from Woodside came rattling down George Street to St Nicholas Street, where Queen Victoria's statue dominated the scene. The phrase "Meet me at the Queen" was familiar to countless courting couples.

The City Fathers, in their infinite wisdom, decided to bury most of St Nicholas Street under a new shopping complex, the St Nicholas Centre. Now the Queen has "flitted" to Queen's Cross (see Walk 9) and the only Royal head you will see is on the back of pound notes dropping from a cash machine in the wall of the Clydesdale Bank. "Markies" (Marks & Spencer) has replaced "Raggie's" – "Raggie" Morrison's, a gloriously old-fashioned store which sold everything from gents' galluses to winter woolies.

It has been claimed that Union Street is one of the earliest and finest fly-overs in the world. Half the street, from the Adelphi to Diamond Street, was artificially created and raised from a minimum of 20 ft (6 m) to more than 50 ft (15 m) above the natural level of the ground. If you find that hard to believe take a look over the railings as you approach St Nicholas churchyard, and look down into the Correction Wynd, which runs under Union Street to the Green.

Past the steps to St Nicholas churchyard is the Facade, 12 Doric columns with an archway in the middle. Designed by John Smith in 1830, it looks at first glance like a granite Folly, but it provides a stylish frontage to St Nicholas kirkyard. The Mither Kirk's graveyard is where the great and the good are buried . . . authors, artists, soldiers, musicians, provosts and poets.

On the left-hand side of the street is the Trinity Centre, a shopping complex whose name is a reminder that it was once Trinity Hall, the magnificent home of the Seven Incorporated Trades. The "Trades" moved to a new Trinity Hall in Holburn Street and a Littlewoods store took its place. The mediaeval hammerbeam roof can still be seen in the store's restaurant.

Back on the right, as you go on past Belmont Street, Kelly's Cats are watching you, 14 of them, sitting on top of Union Bridge. The "cats" are actually leopards. They got their name from Dr William Kelly, the architect who used them as filials when he designed new parapets for the Union Bridge, which was built in its original form in 1805.

Kelly's Cats were also perched on the parapet on the south side of the bridge, but they disappeared when a glossy row of shops were built, blotting out the view to the south. Happily, the view from the north side remains, so you look across Union Terrace Gardens to the Central Library, the South Church, and Her Majesty's Theatre – "Education, Salvation and Damnation" they called it.

Down below, a new dual carriageway cleaves its way up the Denburn. The buildings adjoining Union Street on the east side of the bridge rise up from the depths of the Denburn, well below street level – proof, if any were needed, that Union Street is one of the finest fly-overs in the world.

At the junction of Union Street and Union Terrace is a massive statue of King Edward VII. He has statuesque company. Walk along Union Terrace and

Prince Albert's statue in Union Terrace. William Wallace's statue can be seen behind it.

Robert Burns' statue in Union Terrace.

you will see Rabbie Burns holding his "crimson-tipped" daisy, the Prince Consort holding his plumed hat, and William Wallace holding his hand out as if pointing the way to the Theatre.

Back at the junction, on the opposite side of Union Terrace is the "Monkey House" (the Commercial Union building), which got its nickname because, like the Queen, this was another familiar meeting place. Union Street from the "Monkey House" to Holburn Junction was the most popular stretch of the Mat, although most of the promenading and wolf-whistling was done on the south (Bridge Street) side.

The north side is where the culture and the wealth lie, or so you would think from the names of the streets – Diamond Street, Silver Street, Ruby Lane and Golden Square – although Crown Street is on the south side of Union Street.

At South Silver Street six Ionic columns, 30 ft (9 m) high, form an imposing 90 ft (28 m) frontage to the Music Hall. This is arguably the finest building in Union Street. Designed by Archibald Simpson in 1822, it was known as the Assembly Rooms; the Music Hall was added in 1858. It was originally built by a group of wealthy landowners as a club.

Cross Union Street to Bon Accord Street and go down East Craibstone Street into Bon Accord Square. Bon Accord Terrace and Bon Accord Square were both laid out by Archibald Simpson. The architect built a house for himself and another for his brother in the Square (Nos 13 and 15), but he died in a house in East Craibstone Street.

In a walled-off grassland area in the centre of Bon Accord Square a large, plain granite block commemorates the man who did more than anybody to shape the Granite City – "A Pioneer of Civic Design in his Native City."

At the west end of Bon Accord Square go through West Craibstone Street and turn right up Bon Accord Terrace, crossing Langstane Place and taking you back to Union Street again. The street narrows slightly here, the reason being that it was Union Place before it was swallowed up by Union Street. It was Aberdeen's Harley Street, where many of the city's doctors lived, and to-day it is still regarded as a slightly up-market part of Union Street.

On the left-hand side is the Capital Cinema, which has been a prominent landmark in the Union Street scene for more than half a century. Before that the city's first cinema, the Electric Theatre, stood there.

Union Street ends at Christ's College, built in 1850 to train Free Church ministers. The Free Kirk students patronised Babbie Law's "shoppie", which was at 8 Wellington Place, now part of Holburn Street.

But Union Street gets a benediction from a humbler source. In the Castlegate, at the start of the walk, the Salvation Army Citadel looks down on the market place where the legendary "Cocky" Hunter, King of the second-hand furniture trade in Aberdeen, once sold everything from "a knocker for yer door, or a hoose tae fit yer floor".

To-day, at the other end of Union Street, looking over to Christ's College, is a bar named after him, its entrance stocked with such curiosities as an ancient clock, old mangles, a battered fireplace, and a school desk. Now, thirsty citizens refresh themselves at Cocky Hunter's Bar – toasting, perhaps, "the finest street in the Empire".

So, having Walked the Mat, make your way back to the Castlegate and the Mannie o' the Well.

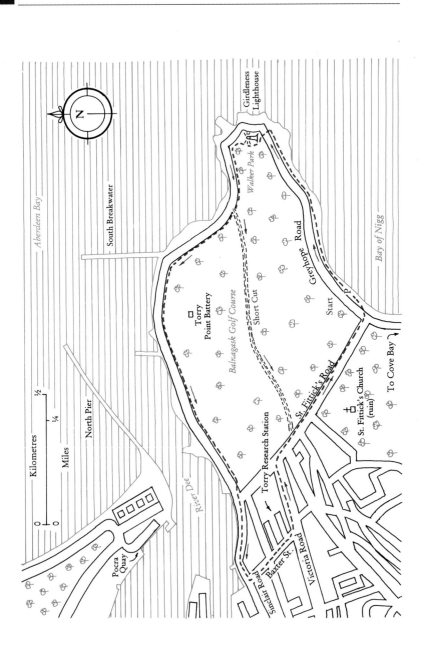

BAY OF NIGG

The townsfolk of Aberdeen once flocked to the Bay of Nigg to cure their ills at a "miracle" well, a superstitious practice that the City Fathers tried to stop. More recently, in pre-war years, people looked after their health in a different way – they turned the Bay into the city's playground, a picnickers' paradise where they could breathe in the sea air.

Nowadays, the Bay is largely deserted. This is where your walk starts, taking in three bays that mark the approach to this bustling oil port. It starts at a car park on the edge of the shore, but if you travel to Nigg by bus you can set out from the Balnagask golf course, a few hundred metres away. There is a bus stop outside the clubhouse.

From the car park the road south goes along the cliffs to Cove, but your route lies on the opposite direction, towards Girdleness Lighthouse. Look for granite steps in a walled area on the left. They lead to Torry's first and only public park – the Walker Park, where the lighthouse keepers grazed their cattle more than a century and a half ago.

Near here you will come upon a different kind of cow, or, as the local dialect has it, a "coo" – the Torry Coo. This was the name given to the Girdleness foghorn, whose melancholy bellow could be heard clear across the city of a foggy night. It stands on the rocks below

INFORMATION

Distance: 4 km (2.5 miles)

Start and finish: Bay of Nigg, From Market Street cross Victoria Bridge to Torry and follow Victoria Road to end of St Fittick"s Road, turning right to the Bay of Nigg. Parking area at the Bay.

Terrain: Easy walking. Pavements and paths all the way. No special footwear needed.

Refreshments: Cafes and shops in Torry.

Public transport: Good bus service from the city centre.

Girdleness Lighthouse.

The Torry Coo.

the 131 ft (39 m) lighthouse, which was built in 1832-33 by Robert Stevenson, grandfather of Robert Louis Stevenson. Sadly, the "coo" has now been silenced and the lighthouse has been automated.

The road goes through a series of bends, and as it straightens out you are looking down on a small but historic inlet called Greyhope Bay. This was where a whaler called the *Oscar* went down in 1813, with the loss of 55 lives. Only two men survived. It was after this disaster that a call went out for a lighthouse, but 20 years passed before it was built.

Harbour from Torry Battery.

The long finger of the South Breakwater is on your right. The road swings round to hug the line of the navigation channel and on your left is the Torry Point Battery, with the date 1861 inscribed over the arched entrance. It was originally armed with 60-pounder guns, but the Battery has rarely fired a shot in anger. It banged away at two unidentified ships in 1941, but they turned out to be friendly.

Near the Battery, above Greyhope Road, there is a car park where motorists come to sit and enjoy an incomparable view of Aberdeen and its sea-front . . . the busy harbour, the wide sweep of Aberdeen Bay, and the spires and steeples that reach up from the grey granite heart of the city. People think of the Bay as a two-mile crescent of sand between the Dee and the Don, but, in fact, from Girdleness to the sands of Forvie in the north, Aberdeen Bay is 13 miles (21km) wide – as one report on Scotland's coastline put it, "one of the longest stretches of beach and dune coastline in Highland Scotland".

Across the channel, cormorants preen themselves on the wall of the North Pier, watching the parade of fishing boats and giant oil ships moving up the channel. Old men and young boys once sat on the pier and fished for saithe, fish which fed on the sewer outlets. There is a link with this in an ugly brick

obelisk on the pier known as Scarty's Monument.
Scarty was a harbour pilot, William Smith, who was a
bit of a character, and his "monument" is, in fact, a
ventilator shaft for one of the sewers.

Leaving the Torry Battery and continuing down
Greyhope Road, you pass the Torry Research Station,
run by the Ministry of Agriculture, Fisheries and Food,
and next door to it is a pub called Campbell's. The
way straight ahead is blocked by a fence and gate
carrying the sign, "Total Oil Marine plc. No
unauthorised entry". Once you could walk down Torry
Quay, for this world of oil and big business was
originally the fishing community of Old Torry, wiped
out when the oilmen came.

Turn left up Baxter Street, passing some old houses
with forestairs, one with the date 1881 on its wall.
Turn left again at the top of Baxter Street, which will
take you on to Victoria Road. Here, on the left, you
pass the Marine Laboratory.

Balnagask golf course stands at the junction of
Victoria Road and St Fittick's Road. There is a bus
stop outside it. The last lap of your walk, however, is
down St Fittick's Road to the car park at the Bay of
Nigg. Here you are on the edge of a little valley called
the Vale of Tullos, which is on your right. Today, the
Vale has been largely buried by housing development.

Over on the grassland on the right is ruined St Fittick's
Church, with a leper's squint, an ancient belfry, and a
walled graveyard full of lurching tombstones. In one
corner of the old kirkyard is the Watch-house used
early last century during the time of the body-snatchers.

St Fittick's Well was in this area. It was here, on the
first Sunday of the year, that people came to drink the
"miracle" waters. In 1630, Aberdeen Kirk Session
censured those who went to the well "in ane
superstitious maner for seeking health thameselffs or
bairnes". One woman is Strathbogie, who sent her
nurse to Nigg with her child, was fined £5 for "washing
the bairn thairin for the recovery of her health".

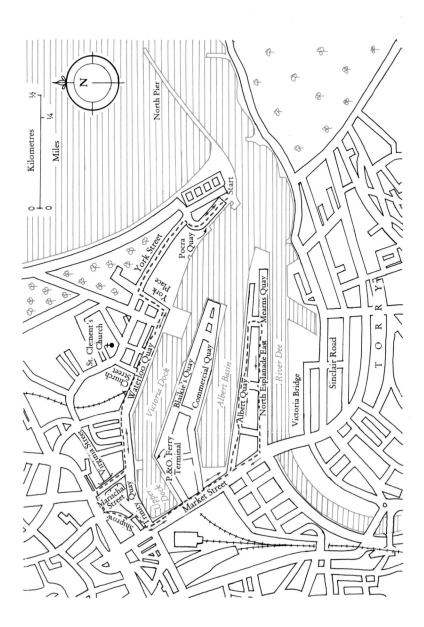

St. Clement's Church

North Pier

York Street

York Place

Pocra Quay

Start

Church Street

Waterloo Quay

Victoria Dock

Virginia Street

Blaikie's Quay

Commercial Quay

Albert Basin

Albert Quay

North Esplanade East

Mearns Quay

River Dee

Victoria Bridge

Sinclair Road

TORRY

P. & O. Ferry Terminal

Marischal Street

Trinity Quay

Upper Dock

Shiprow

Market Street

N

Kilometres

Miles

½

¼

GATEWAY TO THE SEA

Aberdeen Harbour is known as Scotland's Gateway to the North Sea. This walk gives you a glimpse of the bustling port that serves Europe's oil capital. It begins at Pocra Quay, where more than a century ago the whale ships left for the Arctic to hunt for a different kind of oil – whale oil.

The only reminder of the city's whaling days is a rough granite tablet on the quay marking the site of a long-demolished blockhouse, once used as a boiling house for whale oil. Today, huge oil supply ships berth at Pocra – the old Pow Creek, the fishermen's haven – while bulky mud and cement silos loom over the quay. These symbols of the oil age can be seen all over the harbour, brightly painted in a variety of colours.

From Pocra, turn right and then left into York Street. The Craig Ship Repair Yard is on the left, but there are few signs left of Aberdeen's great shipbuilding days. Further along the street is the Neptune Bar, which was shattered by a German bomb when shipyard workers were having a lunchtime drink in July 1940.

Turn left down York Place, where Hall Russell's shipyard once hummed with activity. At one time you could cross from here to Blaikie's Quay by the St Clement's Bridge, but the bridge and the old dock gates were demolished to make way for a new open-plan port to serve the oil industry.

INFORMATION

Distance: 6 km (4 miles)

Start and finish: Pocra Quay, best reached from Beach Boulevard. Parking space at North Pier and on Upper Prom.

Terrain: Easy walking on pavements. No special footwear needed.

Refreshments: Selection of hotels, cafes and pubs in the harbour area.

Public transport: Good bus service from the city centre.

Toilets: On Beach Boulevard and in harbour area.

Opening hours: *Maritime Museum, Shiprow, Mon.-Sat. 1000–1700; Fish market auction sales, from 0700 Mon.-Fri.*

Oil supply vessel in Aberdeen Harbour.

Hall Russell's (originally two companies, Alexander Hall & Co. and Hall, Russell and Co.) is gone but not forgotten. The yards are remembered in the names of two new berths, Hall's Quay and Russell's Quay, built as part of a £12 million development scheme, which utilised the last area of harbour land available for development. As a result, five new quays have been built to meet the port's expanding trade.

Alexander Hall built the first Aberdeen clipper, the *Scottish Maid*, in 1839, a memorable era that is remembered in the third new quay, Clipper Quay. A fourth quay is Duthies Quay, commemorating another famous clipper-building firm, John Duthie, Sons and Co, while the great engineer Thomas Telford, who planned the extension of the North Pier and the deepening of the harbour channel, gives his name to Telford Dock.

There is no entry to the public from Waterloo Quay, but the street itself, and the closes and courts that run off it, hold plenty of interest. One of the major offshore support companies, Seaforth Maritime, has its offices and base here. Watch out for the steeple of St Clement's Church, once the seafarers' kirk, up Church Street; for a well-known drinking howff, Peeps Bar (one of a number of pubs on the quayside); for Theatre Lane, where a plaque records the opening of the Theatre Royal in 1795; and for the magnificent facade of buildings just east of Market Street.

Near Shore Lane is the Old Customs House, an elegant Georgian mansion built in 1771, and next to it Regent House (1898), while on the other side of the lane is the striking architecture of what was John Cook's office, now Inchcape Shipping. The largest building is the granite Harbour Board Office, built in 1883–85, with its distinctive tower and clock dominating the harbour scene.

It is worth taking a detour up Marischal Street, which has many historic associations. When the growth of the harbour made a new approach to it from Castle Street a necessity, the street was cut through the site of what had been for centuries the town house of the

Earls Marischal. Keep an eye open for wall plaques marking the houses where William Dyce, the artist, and William Kennedy, the lawyer and historian, lived.

Marischal Street was the first street in Aberdeen to be paved with "cassies" (square granite setts), and it was carried over Virginia Street, now a dual carriageway, by Bannerman's Bridge. If you look over the bridge on its east side you can see the premises of the ancient Shore Porters' Society, with the dates 1498 (when it was established) and 1897 (when the building was erected) on the wall. The Society is still operating to-day.

Turn left at the top of Marischal Street and along the Castle street to the Shiprow, which curves down to Shore Brae and Trinity Quay. This is one of the oldest streets in Aberdeen. Shipmasters and shore porters lived there – and the town's Provosts. Provost Robert Davidson, the hero of Harlaw, had a tavern in the Shiprow, and John Ross of Arnage, Provost from 1710 to 1712, lived in what is now the Aberdeen Maritime Museum. In the Spring of 1995 work started on an extension to the museum, which will be completed by 1997.

Make your way along Trinity Quay and at the roundabout junction go left up Market Street. There are traffic lights opposite the Market Street entrance to the harbour. Beyond the entrance, Regent Road goes left to the P&O Ferry Terminal. It is from here that the North Sea boats leave for their daily and often stormy runs to Orkney and Shetland. The clock on the Salveson Tower tells you both the time and the temperature, and at the foot of it is a pub called the Quarter Deck.

From the harbour's western perimeter at Market Street the quays push up like long tongues towards the harbour mouth . . . Blaikie's Quay on the south side of Victoria Dock, with Matthews Quay and Commercial Quay turning back along the Albert Basin towards the Fish Market, up again by Albert Quay and back by Mearns Quay and North Esplanade East.

Instead of trawler masts there are the towering silos, blue, yellow, orange, and grey, and instead of trawlers there are mighty stand-by boats with names like *Grampian Sword* and *Grampian Sabre*. Up on the wall of the Fish Market you may see a sign which declares with unintended humour, "Fishing Prohibited", a reminder that the Harbour Board has rod fishing rights.

But oil is king in Aberdeen and the city's once-great fishing industry has gradually diminished. The day of the large trawler is over, and fishing contributes only about 10 per cent of the Harbour Board's revenue on ships and goods. The Board pins its hopes for the future on seine-netters and small inshore trawlers. When the rebuilding of Commercial Quay West and its fish market was completed in 1982 it was described by

Oil supple vessel leaving Aberdeen Harbour.

John R. Turner, former general manager of the Board, as "an act of faith".

For Aberdonians as well as visitors, a trip to the Fish Market is still a colourful spectacle. From 0730 Monday to Friday, you can watch the auction sales there. Parties of visitors, some from abroad, frequently visit the market.

A large part of Aberdeen's history lies within the confines of its port. It is a vivid, exciting place to be – each name has its own story, like Atlantic Wharf, where members of the Royal Family have always disembarked from the Royal yacht on their way to Balmoral.

Huge derricks that can lift 80 tons swing their cargoes on to the quay. There are marine supply firms, fuel companies, fish salesmen, off-shore companies – and Charlie's newsagent and take-away shop. There are rusty old tubs in Albert Basin, a fishing boat called *Jasirene* (who were the James and Irene who gave their names to it?), and a small street with the intriguing name of Midchingle Road. There were Midchingle fishings at one time.

But it is oil that reigns supreme here and as you come down North Esplanade East there is a reminder that drilling for oil is a dangerous game. On the quay is the RGIT Survival Centre, where oil men are trained to survive the rigours and hazards of the North Sea. You can see their training craft bobbing about in the sea off the Prom.

From North Esplanade East you look across the River Dee to Old Torry. It was to Torry that the fisher folk from the coastal villages came for the trawling, so that its population – only 370 in 1843 – began to mushroom. There is little left to remind you of Aul' Torry. Much of it disappeared when the area north of Sinclair Road was cleared to make way for oil installations.

Torry folk regarded themselves as an entirely separate community, and the only link with the town was by a ferry operating across the Dee to Point Law. There is still a Ferry Place near Point Law, between North Esplanade East and Albert Quay.

On 5 April 1876, a local holiday, the ferry was kept busy carrying Aberdeen people to and from Torry, and on one of its trips to the south side of the Dee it was badly overloaded, carrying about 60 people, more than double its normal load. The ferry boat's wire rope broke and the boat capsized. Thirty-three passengers were drowned.

People had talked for a number of years about the need for a bridge over the Dee, and this terrible tragedy speeded things up. The Victoria Bridge was opened in 1881. The bridge marks the turning point of your walk. From here, make your way along Market Street and back by Regent Quay and Waterloo Quay to Pocra.

EEC regulations are likely to result in tightening up of restrictions on public access to the harbour for security and safety reasons. To counter this, the Harbour Board has been considering the possibility of a number of viewing areas. Meantime, you should be alert for signs regarding access and should bear in mind that this is a working harbour.

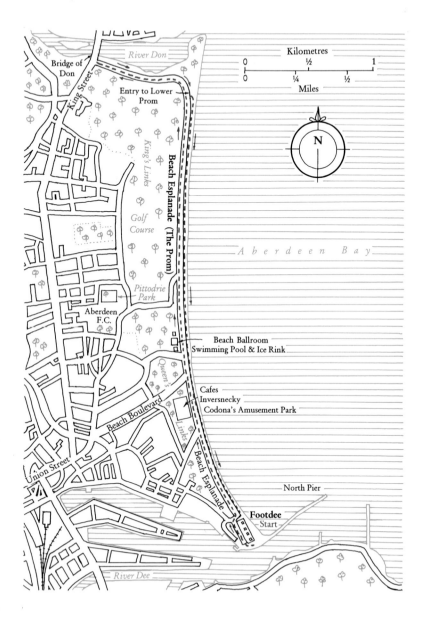

Kilometres

Miles

N

River Don

Bridge of Don

King Street

Entry to Lower Prom

King's Links

Beach Esplanade (The Prom)

Golf Course

Aberdeen Bay

Pittodrie Park

Aberdeen F.C.

Beach Ballroom
Swimming Pool & Ice Rink

Queen's

Cafes
Inversnecky
Codona's Amusement Park

Beach Boulevard

Links

Beach Esplanade

Union Street

North Pier

Footdee
Start

River Dee

THE PROM

Aberdeen's beach promenade runs for two miles along the sea-front, linking the Rivers Dee and Don. A walk on the Prom has become as popular as Walking the Mat (see Walk 1) and for some people it is a trip down memory lane, back to the long-lost days when they listened to the "oompa" bands on the Links, laughed at Harry Gordon in the Pavilion, and sat on deckchairs on the sands.

The starting point of the walk is the old fishing village of Fittie or Futty, a name that last century was corruptly anglicised to Footdee. Two hundred years ago it was a row of thatched cottages, but in 1808–9 it was rebuilt near the North Pier. The North and South Squares came first, followed by the Middle Row and Pilot's Square.

Before setting out it is well worth exploring the old "fisher toun". Look for the Tower of Babylon, a tall building rising above a row of cottages. No one is quite sure how it got its name. Babylon, of course, was a place of depravity, but the Fittie fishers would shy away from such things.

Your route is along the sea-front by the high road – the Beach Esplanade, or upper Prom – and back by the lower promenade. To the left lie the spires and steeples of the city, while to the right is the great sprawl of Aberdeen Bay. Beyond the fence on the opposite side of the road are all that remains of Aberdeen's once-flourishing shipbuilding industry.

INFORMATION

Distance: 6 km (4 miles)

Start and finish: Footdee (Fittie). Main approach is by the Castlegate and Boulevard. Parking at Fittie and on Esplanade.

Terrain: Pavements and tarmac paths. No special footwear needed.

Refreshments: At the Beach Ballroom. There are also restaurants, cafes and shops on the Promenade.

Toilets: At both ends of the walk – at Fittie and the Bridge of Don. Also on the Lower Promenade opposite the Boulevard.

Public transport: Good bus service from the city centre.

Entertainment: Codona's Amusement Park, the Beach Ballroom, the Beach Leisure Centre, with swimming, ice-skating and sports facilities, the Links golf course and golf driving range.

Sand and sea below the Prom.

A Fittie shed, once a fisher's bothy.

Less than half a mile from Fittie is the Prom's busiest section, a line of cafes, ice-cream shops and an amusement arcade. Here, too, was Inversnecky, the mythical home of Harry Gordon, who played to packed houses in the Beach Pavilion. A Continental Cafe stands on the site now and the only reminders of the Laird of Inversnecky's reign are a cafe called Inversnecky and another called the Pavilion. Behind the shops is Codona's Amusement Park, with its dodgem cars, stalls and scenic railway. Back in the 1930s an American called John Iles built a switchback railway, but it was badly damaged by fire in 1940 and demolished shortly afterwards.

Where the Beach Boulevard runs up towards the town centre, two old tramlines can be seen cutting through the Queen's Links. The "trammies" once came rattling down this track from the Castlegate. Near here there was a magnificent bandstand where concerts were held – it cost you two old pennies for a seat. Farther back is the Broad Hill, once known as Cunningar Hill, a name that means "rabbity". It is a mere 94 ft (30 m) in height, but you get a nice view from the top of it.

On the Prom, a fenced-in seating area marks the site of the Beach Shelter, which was topped by a magnificent clock. The City Fathers in their wisdom – and to the annoyance of many Aberdonians – allowed it to deteriorate and finally demolished it.

As you walk along the Prom, you will see adjoining the Beach Ballroom two comparatively new sports centres – a swimming pool and an ice rink. After that, the Kings Links stretch away to the east, most of it given over to an 18-hole golf course. Across the Links is Gallowhill, where a familiar landmark – the city's old gasometer – stood until recently, and near it is Aberdeen FC's ground at Pittodrie. Before Pittodrie became a football pitch it was a dunghill for the city's police horses.

People were kicking a ball on the Links long before the Dons appeared on the scene. James Gordon, Parson of Rothiemay, said it was played on "the fair plaine called the Queen's Lynks in 1661", along with "goffe, bowling and archerie".

"Here lykewayes", said the Parson, "they walk for their health". So encouraged, step along the Prom towards the mouth of the Don. On the left, as you walk, you get a good view over the town.

The road swings to the left as you reach the estuary and runs parallel to the river as far as King Street and the Bridge of Don. Upstream, the river comes tumbling under the ancient Brig o' Balgownie (see Walk 5) before reaching the Don bridge, which was built in 1831 at a cost of about £17,000.

In the 1960s, erosion was so bad at the Beach that it was feared that it would destroy the unprotected dunes, so that the Promenade would have to be abandoned and the invading Spring tides would lap the city. Such a disaster was avoided by laying out a system of groynes along the seafront. A pre-cast coping with promenade walk was also laid down halfway up the dunes. To-day, that "promenade walk" – the lower Prom – is where hundreds of people stroll by the sea.

When you retrace your steps from the Bridge of Don look for an opening taking you on to the lower Prom. It can be seen where the road swings right towards Fittie. There are a number of shelters along the lower Prom and steps down to the sand all the way to Fittie.

The ghosts of yesterday haunt the area near the site of the old Beach Baths. Here were bathing huts and ice-cream stalls, pierrot shows and brass bands . . . and Aberdeen's famous golden sands buried under a mountain of deck-chairs. Now people sit in their cars and watch the sea – or "promenade" along the sea-front.

Site of old Beach Baths, with Beach Ballroom in background.

On the last leg of the walk you can see the North Pier poking its long finger out to sea and in the distance the silhouette of the Torry Battery on Balnagask. Then you are back at Fittie, having completed your Walk on the Prom.

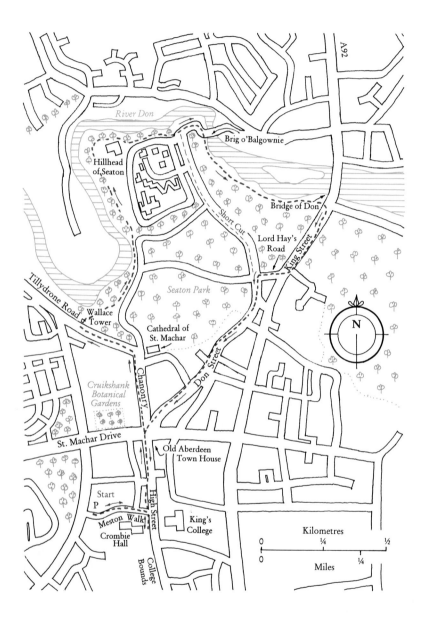

River Don

Brig o'Balgownie

Hillhead of Seaton

Bridge of Don

Short Cut

Lord Hay's Road

King Street

Seaton Park

Tillydrone Road

Wallace Tower

Cathedral of St. Machar

N

Chanonry

Cruikshank Botanical Gardens

Don Street

St. Machar Drive

Old Aberdeen Town House

Start
P

High Street

Meston Walk

King's College

Crombie Hall

College Bounds

A92

Kilometres

0   ¼   ½

0   ¼

Miles

AULTON AND SEATON

The distance between the two market crosses of New Aberdeen and Old Aberdeen was once said to be a "large Scottish mile". The route followed the old high road to the north, up the Gallowgate to Mounthooly and over the Spital Brae to College Bounds and the High Street. To-day that "Scottish mile" represents a giant step into the past.

History is on your heels on almost every corner of the Aulton. Our approach is from the car park at Meston Walk, but before heading up the High Street turn right into College Bounds, where two curious minarets adorn the huge Powis Lodge gate at the entrance to the Crombie Hall of Residence. The minarets were erected by John Leslie, a young laird of Powis, as a tribute to Lord Byron.

Turning back from College Bounds into the High Street, King's College and its Chapel are on your right, opposite Meston Walk. The complex of buildings that make up "King's" today is dominated by its magnificent Crown Tower. On the lawn beneath it is the bronze and marble monument to William Elphinstone, Bishop of Aberdeen, who founded King's College in 1498.

From the High Street, where a sign points the way to the King's College Conference and Visitor's Centre, you can made your way through the quadrangle to the restaurant and souvenir shop that form part of the centre.

Since No. 1 is the logical place to start a walk down the High Street, take a look at the two-storey house at the corner of Meston Walk, whose door lintel carries the name "College Place". See if you can guess the meaning of the curious sign – a gilt sun – on the wall. In fact, it shows that a private insurance company once did business there.

Across the grounds on the right is Elphinstone Hall, while on the pavement is a striking gateway to both old and new . . . to New King's and to the Old Brewery. Beer from the Old Brewery, which is now a University department, once went out from the

INFORMATION

Distance: 5 km (3 miles)

Start and finish: Car park at Meston Walk, off Bedford Road. From here it is only a few minutes walk to the High Street.

Terrain: Good walking, but path from Seaton Park to the Brig o' Balgownie can be muddy in wet weather. Also, river path from the Brig o' Balgownie to Bridge of Don has a steep climb at the start. Alternative route by Don Street advisable for unfit or elderly people. Strong footwear recommended.

Public transport: Good bus service from the city centre.

Refreshments: Excellent restaurant in Visitor's Centre at King's College. There is also a cafe in the High Street used by students.

Toilets: In High Street near St Machar Drive and in Seaton Park.

Opening hours: *King's College, St Machar's Cathedral:* open daily 0900–1700; *Cruickshank Botanic Garden:* open all year Mon-Fri 0900–1630, May-Sept. Sat-Sun 1400–1700; *Brig o' Balgownie.*

Entrance to New King's.

Aulton to Balmoral Castle. The name is also perpetuated in nearby Brewery Lane.

Much of the fascination of the Aulton lies in its wynds, courts and closes. Some have gone, among them a handful of Wynds. Reid's Wynd, for instance, "a broad green way to the Links for the use of the clergy", and Beverly's Wynd, Wagril's Wynd, Bartlet's Wynd and College Wynd. Duncan's Wynd is still there, as are Thom's Court, Greenlaw Court and Church Walk, beside St Mary's Free Church, now occupied by the geography department.

The restored Mercat Cross stood outside St Mary's at one time, but now it has been moved to a more appropriate spot in front of the Town House. If King's College crowns one end of High Street, the old Town House crowns the other. This late 18th century Georgian building, three storeys high, has a clock tower topped by a cupola. Over the entrance is the burgh coat-of-arms, dated 1721.

Barely noticeable across the road from the Town House is Market Lane, a link with the old Aulton Fair, or St Luke's Fair. Nearby Baillie Place recalls the former burgh status of Old Aberdeen.

Before you leave the High Street and cross to the Chanonry take a look at the house round the corner at 60 St Machar Drive – Cluny's Port. The St Machar Cathedral precincts were enclosed by four ports or gateways and Cluny's Port, originally called Chanonry Port, was the south gateway. It was the gatehouse to Cluny's Gardens, now the Cruickshank Botanical Gardens, on the other side of St Machar Drive. They are well worth a visit.

The Chanonry runs its stately tree-lined way to St Machar's Cathedral. Its large, dignified houses mostly belong to the 18th or early 19th centuries. In sharp contrast is No. 9. This is Mitchell's Hospital, originally built in 1801 "to clothe and maintain five widows and five unmarried daughters of Merchant and Trade Burgesses of Old Aberdeen". Note the sundial in the court.

No. 13, almost opposite the main gateway of the Cathedral, is Chanonry Lodge, the home of the Principal of the University. Here, the Chanonry takes a right-angle turn and runs down to Don Street. No. 20 is Chaplain's Court, whose moulded pend arch is surmounted with the arms of Bishop Gavin Dunbar, who built the original Chaplain's Court in 1519.

The great fortified church of St Machar's Cathedral, dating back to the 14th century, rises over the Chanonry, its twin spires known to every Aberdonian and to thousands of visitors. In its graveyard lie the great and the good – and some, perhaps, not quite so good. Margery Laing is among them. Margery, whose single name was May Gray, was nursemaid to Lord Byron. It is said that when he was a young man she seduced him and was sacked and sent home from England in disgrace.

From the Cathedral, at the entrance to Seaton Park, your route lies up Tillydrone Road. This "cassied" road, which was the old route to the north, takes you to Benholm's Lodging, better known to Aberdonians as the Wallace Tower, although it had no connection with the Scots hero. In 1963 it was taken down from its site in the Netherkirkgate and rebuilt stone by stone on Tillydrone Hill.

The grassy mound at the summit of the hill is the Motte of Tillydrone, the site of a 12th century fort commanding a ford over the River Don. From the Wallace Tower, make your way down a path leading into the park, following it along the right bank of the River Don.

First, however, take a look round the park. The name "Seaton" means "peaceful retreat", and that is what it is. It was less peaceful in the 19th century, when it was used as a racecourse. The last race was run in 1928. Now you can stroll in its sheltered rose gardens, take the youngsters to the railway wagons and the brake van in the adventure playground, or walk by the river.

The path by the Don rises high above the tree-lined gorge of Balgownie. Swans, mallards and moorhens can be seen on the grassy flats of the river, whose dark waters surge away towards the old Brig o' Balgownie. On the right of the path is the students' residence at Hillhead of Seaton.

The path comes out on Don Street, near the Brig o' Balgownie. If you want to cut short the walk, turn right when you leave the park and follow Don Street back to St Machar Drive and down the High Street to Meston Walk, but before you do so, go left for a short distance for a look at the old Brig. The alternative route is by a path along the river to the Bridge of Don.

When you leave Seaton Park the first house on your left is the Chapter House (it is, incidentally, misnamed), which has the initial G.C. and B.H. and the date 1655 over an arched pend with a coat of arms. G.C. was George Cruickshank, who built the house, and B.H. was his wife, Barbara Hervie.

Nearby is the Balgownie Mission Hall, and where the cobbled road turns right, a group of other houses add to the old world charm of this corner by the Don. The famous Brig o' Balgownie, built in the late 13th and early 14th centuries, completes the picture. The brig has been rightly described as "one of the most hauntingly beautiful Gothic survivals in Scotland".

Brig o' Balgownie.

Beyond the Brig is the Cot Town of Balgownie, whose ancient red-tiled cottages were restored by a private developer. The house nearest the Brig, built about 1600, was originally known as the Black Nook Alehouse. It took its name from the Black Nook Port, a dark pool to the west of the bridge, where evil spirits are said to have lured passers-by to their deaths.

The centuries slipped away and the ancient bridge settled into its niche in the history books while a new bridge was built over the Don. This was completed in 1830 and cost £16,000. To get to the Bridge of Don take a path near the Balgownie bridge where a sign says "Nether Don". It drops down towards the river, then climbs steeply up above it, passing a big display panel which tells you all about the Donmouth Nature Reserve, its sand dunes, salt marsh and birds.

The path comes out at the south end of the Bridge of Don, where you turn right and walk down King Street to Lord Hay's Road, a short road leading to the Don Street entrance to Seaton Park. Here you turn left up Don Street, which was once known as Seatongate, the "gait" or way to Seaton. Its picturesque houses also have their stories – No. 78, for instance, carries the name Bishop's Port, although the Bishop's Port or East Port was actually on the other side of the street.

In Clark's Lane, adjoining the west gable of the Bishop's Port, are four single-storey cottages with red-tiled roofs and roses round the doors.

The Dower House is at No. 49, built on the side of the Cathedral treasurer's house, and Bede House built in 1676, is at Nos. 20 and 22. This old building, which has a projecting tower and a corbelled stair turret, is now let to municipal tenants and is known as Bede House Court.

Leaving Don Street you cross St Machar Drive to the High Street and make your way back to the car park in Meston Walk, leaving behind the sights and sounds of an ancient community whose beauty will linger long in your mind.

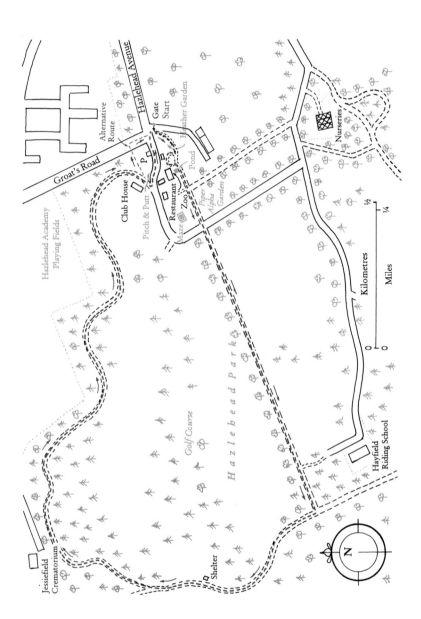

HAZLEHEAD

When Aberdeen Town Council bought the 852-acre estate of Hazlehead in 1920, a letter to the local paper criticised the move and complained that people were "already under a burden of taxation unprecedented in the history of this country". The cost was just £40,000.

Seventy years later, this walk shows you what Aberdonians got for their money. The starting point is the car park at the junction of Groats Road and Hazlehead Avenue. Directly opposite is the entrance to the park, beside a small Tudor-style cottage. There are steps down to the cottage and you can enter the park this way or by the main gate.

When you enter the park ignore for the moment the path on the right, which leads to a big red-roofed shelter. Instead, follow the path ahead of you. It curves round past a row of beech trees and takes you to the park's heather garden. Heather is always regarded as Scotland's own special plant, but there are varieties in the garden from as far afield as Spain and Italy. You'll also see some lucky white heather there!

From the heather garden you can cut through to the path from the gate. Almost adjacent to the shelter is the entrance to Hazlehead's miniature zoo, where there is a free-flying aviary, a small aquarium, rabbits, donkeys and ducks . . . shelducks, teal ducks, pin-tail ducks, ring-tail ducks. The kids will love it.

INFORMATION

Distance: 6 km (3½ miles)

Start and finish: Car park at entrance to Hazlehead Park, another near golf clubhouse.

Terrain: Good walking, although the track in the woodland section of the route can be muddy in wet weather.

Refreshments: Cafe in Hazlehead Park, open Apr.-Sept. 1000–1700.

Public transport: Good bus service from the city centre.

Toilets: In the park.

Clydesdales at work in Hazlehead.

Leaving the zoo you come to a polished red-granite fountain, while the park restaurant can be seen a short distance ahead. The restaurant, with its Continental-style patio, pool and fountain, was built in 1960 on the site of the old Hazlehead House, home of William Rose, an Aberdeen shipowner, who bought the estate in 1775.

"Bruce and Spider" stone.

When Aberdeen Town Council bought the estate in 1920 they were in a sense buying back their own land, for Hazlehead was part of the vast territory known as the Freedom Lands, gifted to the town by King Robert the Bruce in 1319. The link with Bruce is recalled in a series of cairns near the restaurant. Each has a historical scene carved on it . . . Bruce at Bannockburn, Bruce and the Spider, and Bruce presenting the Freedom Lands to the citizens of Aberdeen.

The cairns are just beyond the restaurant and a little further on is the maze. People have been getting lost behind its towering privet hedges since 1935, when it was gifted to the city by Sir Henry Alexander, a former Lord Provost. Don't worry, there's a watcher there to keep an eye on you if you can't find your way out.

Piper Alpha memorial.

Directly opposite the maze, across the main path through the park, is the North Sea Memorial Garden, recalling the tragic day in July 1988, when 167 men were killed on the Piper Alpha oil platform 208 km (129 miles) offshore in the North Sea. Only 61 men were rescued. The sculpted figures of three oil men stand out starkly on top of the memorial in the centre of the garden.

Next to the Piper Alpha garden is another rose garden – the Queen Mother Rose Garden, commemorating the royal lady's 80th birthday.

What appears to be a trio of standing stones are grouped together in one of the gardens. In fact, these giant stone slabs were intended to be sculpted into granite lions for the King George VI Bridge over the

River Dee, which was opened in 1941. The plan was dropped and in 1970 they were taken to Hazlehead and given the name Hazlehenge.

Near the west boundary of the park, where you go through a gate, cross a minor traffic road, and continue on a tarmacadam track stretching ahead between the fairways of Hazlehead golf course. As you get near the top of the road you pass a track going left to Hayfield riding school.

A little way ahead is a T-junction. Turn right and you come to another junction marked by a triangle of grass with a few trees on it. You'll find a drinking fountain here and also a seat where you can take a breather and watch the golfers driving down the 12th hole.

Go left at the junction and follow the path as it runs parallel with the 12th hole towards a green shelter in the distance. Bear left again at the shelter. The track swings left, but your route is by a narrower track going off to the right and into the woods.

You come eventually to a corner where the trees open out and you are running parallel with another track on your left, the two tracks being separated by an "island" of trees. Note the dry-stane dykes – they were built at least a century ago. Behind them is an area of parkland where young trees have been planted and paths laid out.

From the track you get an interesting view over the city, picking out the Woodend Hospital clock tower and the communication mast on Anderson Drive. The fairways are in front of you again and you turn sharp left, passing the 18th tee. Look down the fairway and you will see the "19th Hole" – Hazlehead Golf Club.

The track wanders past Hazlehead Academy playing fields and ends up behind the clubhouse. Go round it and follow the road back to the car park opposite the entrance to Hazlehead.

Alternatively, go left down a tree-lined path which passes the caravan park entrance on Groat's Road. Turn right down Groat's Road and the car park is a short distance ahead.

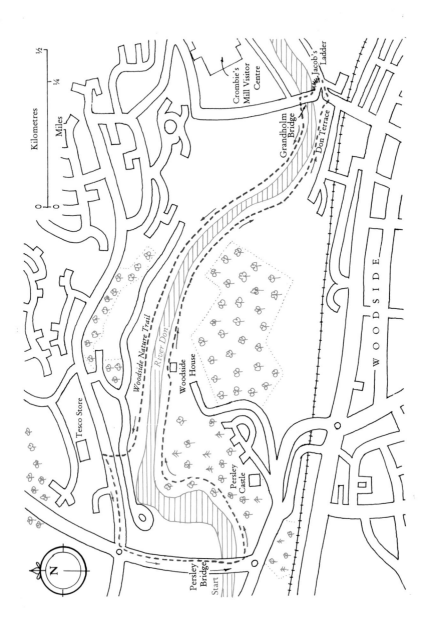

PERSLEY AND GRANDHOLM

A ladder to heaven awaits the walker on the Woodside nature trail in Aberdeen. The trail links two well-known bridges – Persley and Grandholm – and it runs along the banks of the River Don, whose mighty waters were once harnessed for the mills that operated in the Grandholm area.

The starting point is Persley Bridge. From the north side of the river, near the Tesco store, cross the bridge on the left-hand pavement and keep an eye open for a stone at the end of the bridge marked "49 S". This is a March Stone, one of 67 which mark the Freedom Lands of Aberdeen, granted to the town by Robert the Bruce in the 14th century.

Where the road curves away from the bridge, take a wide track which cuts off to the left. It runs towards the river and then climbs up to the right. If you continue along it you will find yourself at the entrance to a large imposing building which was at one time known locally as Persley Castle.

Half-hidden in the trees high above the Don, its castellated structure speaks of a romantic past, but there was no spirit of romance when this fort-like building was erected. It also became known as "The Barracks", for it was built to house children who were used as sweated labour in a calico-printing business.

The building, which was erected at the beginning of last century, eventually became a sawmill. To-day it is a home for old people.

There was a snuff mill upstream from the Barracks at one time, but it was closed down when an Act of Parliament

INFORMATION

Distance: 4 km (2½ miles)

Start and finish: Persley Bridge. From the roundabout at the junction of North Anderson Drive and Great Northern Road go down Mugiemoss Road and, crossing Persley Bridge, turn up the Parkway. Turn right at the Parkway roundabout and park your car near the Tesco Superstore on Laurel Drive.

Terrain: The tracks and footpaths vary on the walk; some sections require a certain amount of care. No special footwear is required.

Refreshments: There is a coffee shop at the Crombie Mill Visitor Centre. The Centre is open Mon.-Sat. 0900–1630, Sun. 1200–1630 all year round.

Public transport: Good bus service from the city centre.

Toilets: At Crombie's Visitor Centre.

The Fort.

prohibited snuff mills from operating within three miles (5 km) of the sea. There were also waulk, bleachfield, calico-printing and cotton mills, and all along this stretch of the Don are reminders of the trail's industrial past.

The road to the Barracks is a dead-end, but on the left of the track is a ruined house with arched windows. This was the gatehouse – and it is our "gateway" to Grandholm. A narrow path runs down the side of the building and round the front before dropping steeply to the riverside. There is an alternative way down at the other gable-end, where steps lead to the path.

Machinery from old
Grandholm Works on display
on Persley walk.

Running parallel to the riverside path is the dried-up channel of the Upper Mill Lade, which brought water to the machinery of Woodside Works, where cotton manufacture was introduced to Aberdeen in 1779. By 1822 more than 3000 people were employed there. It closed in 1851.

Broken walls, sluice gates, mill lades . . . Nature softens these relics of the mills whose lifeblood came from the Don. At one grassy clearing there are two giant links with the old cotton factory at Woodside. Two huge flywheels, supported by stanchions, dominate this peaceful rural scene. The wheels, water-powered by the mill lade, turned the factory machinery. An even bigger 75-ton wheel, built for Grandholm Mills, was sent to the Royal Scottish Museum.

As you head along the trail towards Grandholm, past some ruins, you can see Grandholm Bridge in the distance. At its south end is Jacob's Ladder, its narrow steps rising up to Don Terrace. Its name was inspired by the Old Testament story of how Jacob saw in a dream a ladder reaching up to heaven.

Maybe it had its own special meaning for the thousands of Grandholm workers who struggled up its 66 steps at the end of a hard day's work to reach their "heaven" on earth – their homes in the villages of Cot-town, Tanfield and Printfield, which were later combined to form the burgh of Woodside. To-day there are two Jacob's Ladders. The old "ladder" is closed off and overgrown. The modern "ladder", still in use, has 97 steps, but they are 4 m wide and go up in stages, making it much easier to ascend.

When you cross Grandholm Bridge, you can see a footbridge further upstream. On the north side of the main bridge a road goes right where a sign says "J. & J. Crombie, Ltd., Grandholm Mills", while a larger sign indicates "Museum and Mill Shop".

Crombies, who had a mill at Cothal, or Little Fintray, took over Grandholm in 1859. Today the name Crombie is known throughout the world and the Visitor Centre is well worth seeing. An audio-visual show turns the pages back on Grandholm's past . . . on the mill girls of the Twenties and Thirties, and on the Grandholm Big Wheel, the biggest water wheel in the world, which was 8 m in diameter, 6m wide, and used 115,000 cubic feet of water per minute. It was demolished in 1905.

The famous Crombie cloth can be seen – and bought – in the mill shop, and there is a coffee shop where you can have a cuppa before setting off on the return leg of the walk. Go back to the bridge, where you will see on the opposite side of the road a sign saying "Crombie Football Club". From here a path goes left towards the river.

The path rises and falls in places, with side tracks, mostly used by fishermen, branching off to the river. Take the right-hand path – the "high" road – you'll find it easier.

For part of the way the path sticks closely to a fence and where the fence ends there is a steep, sandy drop to a bigger track. It is difficult and slippery, but it can be avoided by going a little left and following an easier route.

Once on the main track you will see a lade on your right and a path crossing it. This takes you out on to the road near Tesco, but to complete the nature trail carry straight on, following the river, until you come to some sluice gates. From here it is only a short distance to a side road below Tesco – the end of the walk.

Across the Don to Tesco supermarket.

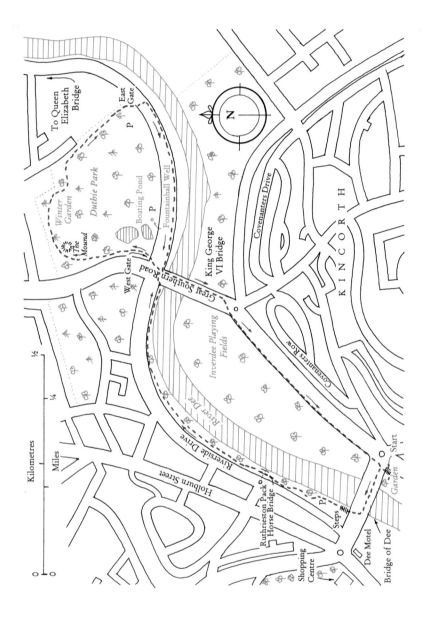

THE DEE AND DUTHIE PARK

When you set out on this walk, first check the time – not on your watch, but on a sundial. You'll find it on steps leading from Aberdeen's Bridge of Dee into a pleasant garden on the west side of the bridge. On it you can see the date 1719 and a curious set of initials – AWMROBW. These are the initials of Alexander Watson, who was elected Master of Bridge Works (MROBW) in 1718, holding the office for a year.

The sundial was put on the bridge when repairs were carried out in 1719, but for a long time it was useless, for the iron gnomon, the arm which projects the shadow on to the sundial, disappeared last century. It was eventually replaced.

The roar of traffic rises above the bridge, but, whatever the sundial shows, time really stands still in this quiet little garden. It is the starting point of a walk embracing three bridges, two ancient, one modern. Once the site of a coach house, the garden sits on the path of the Causey Mounth, the old route south from Aberdeen.

History has left its mark on the old brig. It bears a tremendous collection of coats of arms and commemorative inscriptions, the oldest going back to 1520. One stone carries the inscription, "Gavin Dunbar caused me to be built over the River Dee, AD 1525". Gavin Dunbar was the Bishop who saw the bridge through to its final completion in 1527. Some of the crests can be seen from the garden, others from the north bank of the river.

Climb up the steps past the sundial and walk to the north end of the bridge. Keeping one eye on the traffic, cross the road and go down another set of steps to the riverside. Here, you join a path that follows the Dee on its way to the sea.

As you begin the walk you can see the bridge's seven semi-circular ribbed arches. It has been described as

INFORMATION

Distance: 4 km
(2½ miles)

Start and finish:
Bridge of Dee. Your car can be parked on Riverside Drive, which can be entered just before crossing the Bridge of Dee from Holburn Junction, or from Riverside Gardens, off Holburn Street.

Terrain: Footpaths or pavements. No special footwear needed.

Refreshments: Tearoom in Duthie Park, open 1000–1700 all year round.

Public transport: Good bus service from the city centre.

Toilets: in Duthie Park.

Aberdeen's finest single monument of the Middle Ages. At one time it had a chapel for wayfarers and a great port or gateway.

Across the river, the housing estate of Kincorth climbs up the Hill of Kincorth, some of its streets carrying names like Covenanters Row, Covenanters Drive, Faulds Gate and Faulds Row. They mark a site called Covenanters' Faulds, where the camp fires of the Covenanting Army blazed on the eve of the Battle of the Bridge of Dee in 1639:

> Upon the 18th day of June
> A dreary day to see,
> The southern lords did pitch their camp
> Just at the Bridge of Dee.

In the spring, the grassy banks on the north side of the river are bright with daffodils, stretching away in a golden carpet towards the Dee estuary. Up on your left is Riverside Drive, planned in 1875 as a broad carriage drive next to the river. The Park Hotel, Ruthrieston School and the Church of Scotland's imposing Deeford hostel are three prominent buildings on the Drive.

The river curves through a historic area where Ruadri, a Celtic Mormaer of Mar, had a motte and bailey stronghold overlooking the ford where travellers crossed the Dee. Ruthrieston – *Ruddreistoun* – once had an annual fair, but now the old hamlet has vanished into the granite maw of the city. There is still

The old Pack bridge.

a link with the past in an old Pack Bridge built in 1693–94 to span the Ruthrieston Burn. It was built without parapets so that pack-horses could get over it without difficulty.

Like the Bridge of Dee it is decorated with heraldic panels and inscriptions. One panel was the cause of a row between the Provost and the City Fathers. Provost Robert Cruickshank, whose daughter married Alexander Watson, the Master of Works at the Bridge of Dee, annoyed the magistrates by putting his coat of arms up on the bridge without permission. When he was no longer Provost they took down the stone, cut another inscription on the reverse side, and stuck it back on the bridge. Seven years later the stone was restored to its original position.

The pack-bridge was shifted 30 metres to the east in 1923 and rebuilt with parapets, which destroyed its original character. It is not much of a brig, but when you cross it you can pause and remind yourself that you are standing on centuries of Aberdeen history.

So it is over the old Pack Bridge and down the river path to the fisherman's bothy and the third bridge, which is about 800 m from the Bridge of Dee. The King George VI Bridge, opened in 1941, was intended to take traffic away from the Bridge of Dee, but half a century later, while the planners argue about yet another bridge, cars and lorries are still jamming its 16th century predecessor.

The George VI Bridge was opened by Queen Elizabeth, now the Queen Mother, who had the pawky Lord Provost Sir Tommy Mitchell at her side. Tommy forgot his lines and said to the Queen Mother in an audible whisper, "I'm afraid of making a hash of this!" Further downstairs is another Royal bridge, the Queen Elizabeth Bridge, opened in 1983.

The path takes you to the traffic roundabout at the north end of the George VI Bridge. From here you cross to the West Gate of Duthie Park, which lies at the corner of Riverside Drive and Great Southern

One of the Duthie Park boating ponds.

Road. The route now circles the park before returning to Riverside Drive by the East Gate.

There are three park roads stretching out from the West Gate entrance. The avenue on the right goes down to a car park and a boating pond, and just beside the car park is an old ivy-covered well. This is the Fountainhall Well, which three centuries ago played an important role in the city's water supply. It was taken from its original site and rebuilt at the Duthie Park in 1903.

The middle road from the West Gate runs down to a pond spanned by a large bridge. The pond is one of three linked ponds where ducks and moorhens paddle about, snooze on the islands, or come ashore for titbits. Paddleboats for youngsters can be hired on the higher pond. This is a lovely corner of the park.

There are toilets just beyond the top pond. Go left from here and ahead you will see a small red and grey granite fountain, the Temperance Fountain ("Thou gavest them water for their thirst", says the inscription, but the water has dried up). From the fountain go left up a grassy space between trees and turn right at the war memorial – in front of you is the Mound.

This grassy knoll, which is a blaze of colour in summer, was originally intended to take the largest flagpole in the North of Scotland. That novel idea never came off, so the next plan was to put William Wallace's statue on top of it. Wallace, however, landed up in Union Terrace. In the end, a flagpole was erected on the Mound. Sadly, it could never claim to be the biggest in the North.

Follow the road at the foot of the Mound until you come to the famous Winter Gardens. With a wealth of tropical plants, sculptures, curios and antiquities, the gardens are immensely popular with both visitors and local people. The exhibits range from Kelly's Cats, which once decorated the south side of Union Bridge, to the wheelbarrow used when Duthie Park's first turf was cut in August, 1881.

In the Winter Gardens.

From the Winter Gardens you look across the parkland to a splendid Victorian bandstand, a silent monument to the days of the brass bands. Further on is a tall red granite obelisk erected in honour of Sir James McGrigor, Director General of the Army Medical Department in the Peninsular War.

Next to the Winter Gardens is the tearoom and beyond it a road circles the park and goes down past a statue dedicated to Elizabeth Crombie Duthie, who gifted the park to the city. This road leads to the East Gate, which is near the boating pond. From the East Gate cross to the pavement on the south side of Riverside Drive, walk to the roundabout, and turn left on to the bridge. Once over it, cross to the west side and make your way along Great Southern Road to the Bridge of Dee. The Inverdee playing fields are on your right, Kincorth on your left.

The last building before the Bridge of Dee is a hotel called the Ghillies Lair. Turn right on the bridge and back to where your car is parked on Riverside Drive.

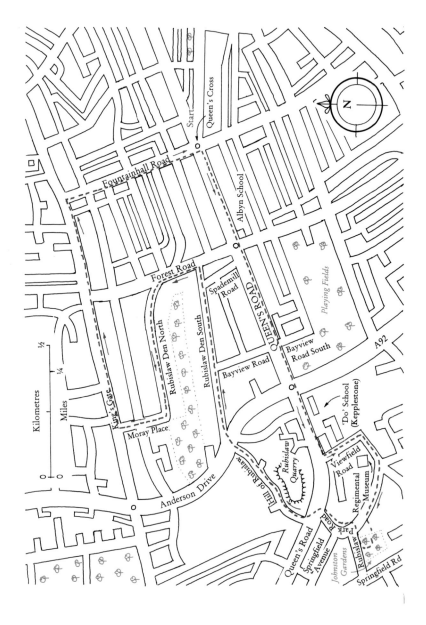

THE WEST END

Queen Victoria stands on a granite pedestal in the middle of a busy Aberdeen traffic roundabout, looking west towards her beloved Balmoral. Her statue at Queen's Cross is on the edge of the city's West End, an area which has been likened to the New Town of Edinburgh. Its wide roads and tree-lined streets are reminiscent of Auld Reekie's Georgian squares and crescents.

Here is what one town planner called "a superb example of the 19th century design for gracious living". Much of that gracious living came from the stone which, blasted from the depths of Rubislaw Quarry, was used to build the Granite City.

The walk begins at Queen's Gardens, in the north corner of Queen's Cross, under the regal gaze of Queen Victoria. The Gardens, which have terraced houses with two continuous wrought-iron balconies at first-floor level, ease you into Queen's Road.

Now you face what the Lallans poet, Alastair Mackie, called "the granite grandery" of this magnificent street, with "grand hooses on ilkie side aa the wey up". One

INFORMATION

Distance: 6 km (3½ miles)

Start and finish: Queen's Cross. Street parking in Queen's Road and neighbouring streets.

Toilets: Johnston Gardens.

Refreshments: Abundance of hotels, restaurants and pubs in Queen's Road.

Public transport: Good bus service from the city centre.

Opening Hours: *Gordon Highlanders Regimental Museum:* Tues & Thurs. 1300–1645, third Sun 1400–1600 (check times – Tel: 318174); *Johnston Gardens.*

Queen's Cross

Granite head of Queen Victoria.

of the first "hooses" is the Grampian Enterprise offices at No. 10, and if you look carefully you will see Queen Victoria waiting to greet you – or, at anyrate, her head.

Lying at the foot of the steps into the building is a sculptured stone head of the Queen. Nobody seems to know where it came from, although some people say it was at Queen's Cross before her statue was erected there.

Across the road is a well-known hostelry, the Dutch Mill, and next to it the Cafe Society, a Continental-type eating place, while a little further on is Albyn School. A century ago a hamlet called Barefold stood there. At the corner of Spademill Road, on the opposite side of Queen's Road, is the old toll-house, now a licensed grocer's shop.

Spademill Road is a quiet tree-lined street running up to Rubislaw Den South. It was part of an old route leading to the Stocket and the Skene road, passing a small cot-town whose red-tiled cottages were smothered in flowers and evergreens. Its name might have been plucked from a storybook – Hirpletillim. Until 1857 there was a distillery near here – Glenburnie Distillery – and Spademill Road took its name from the wooden spades used for turning the barley during the whisky-making.

The gloss has been slightly dimmed in the "grand grandery" of Queen's Road by the conversion of many of the houses of commercial premises, doctors' surgeries and solicitors' offices, but the most striking of them all, No. 50, remains in private hands. This was the home of John Morgan, a prominent Aberdeen builder, who was largely responsible for the laying out of Union Terrace Gardens.

There have been differing views on No. 50, which was designed by Morgan's partner, John Bridgeford Pirie. It has been described as "a masterpiece", and "amazing baroque edifice", and "another of Pirie's bizarre Victorian domestic villas". It is certainly eye-catching.

Just before reaching Anderson Drive, you pass
Bayview Road, which at one time marked the western
end of the built-up area. It was originally known as Bay
View because from it you could catch a glimpse of the
sea away to the south-east. On the other side of the
street, Bayview Road South runs down the edge of the
Grammar School playing fields.

At Anderson Drive, cross to the south side of the road,
where the old "Do School" (College of Domestic
Science), now called Kepplestone, is on you left. Turn
left opposite the petrol station in Queen's Road and go
down Viewfield Road. On your right is the entrance to
St Luke's, the Regimental Headquarters and Museum
of the Gordon Highlanders.

It is well worth a visit (for times see Information).
Watch out for a large piece of granite just inside the
date. An inscription on it tells you that the stone is
from one of the Barrack blocks destroyed in April
1942, when the Germans bombed the Gordon
Barracks at the Bridge of Don, home of the Regiment
from 1935 to 1960.

St Luke's was the studio of Sir George Reid, President
of the Royal Scottish Academy. Before that it was
called Kepplestone Cottage, but in 1880 it was
extended by Dr William Kelly, the architect who gave
Kelly's Cats to the city. These were the leopard finials
decorating the north parapet of Union Bridge (see
Walk 1).

Viewfield Road runs down to the foot of the hill, goes
sharp right and then bears left. Look for a sign,
"Johnstone Gardens". Aberdeen is well served with
parks, but this is the jewel of them all. Here, small
really is beautiful. Streams, waterfall, rockeries, rustic
bridges leading over ponds where mallard, muscovy
ducks and moorhens splash among the water irises . . .
it is sheer delight.

After walking through the park you can leave it by the
rear entrance. A track from the back gate puts you
back on your route. Bear right past Springfield Avenue

Johnstone Gardens.

and go up Rubislaw Park Road to Queen's Road. Go left on Queen's Road and at the lights a short distance ahead turn right up the Hill of Rubislaw.

This was where the Granite City had its birth pangs. It is said that half of Aberdeen came out of Rubislaw Quarry, which is 465 ft (141 m) deep, 900 ft (274 m) long and 750 ft (228 m) wide. Its blue-grey granite was used in public work projects all over the country, but in 1969 it became uneconomic and was closed down.

Sadly, the nearest you will get to the quarry is a fearsome fence swathed in barbed wire, which is on your right as you walk over the Hill. Spaced out along it are huge yellow signs carrying the warning – DANGER. There was a time when you could peer down into the Big Hole, but no longer. The Hill itself houses the offices of some of the city's major oil companies.

Follow the pavement over the Hill and you will come out on Anderson Drive. Cross the street and you are at the top of Rubislaw Den South (no entry for traffic) and here you will see Rubislaw granite at its best. To Aberdonians, Rubislaw was where the toffs lived. People came here on their ritual Sunday stroll to gape and gawk and marvel at how the other half lived. Comedians made fun of it. Harry Gordon often tilted at the nobs and snobs in the Elysian suburbs of Rubislaw.

The Den is a street of grey granite and pink granite, of copper beech trees, rhododendron bushes, roses round the door and smooth well-kept lawns. Or, as Alastair

Mackie put it, of "trig rockeries" and "privet hedgeraws burstin thro the jile bars of their black railings".

As you go down towards Bayview Road you can actually see the distant glitter of Aberdeen Bay. At No. 24 you are at Hirpletillim, or, at anyrate, where it was before fashionable granite villas sprouted in the shadow of Rubislaw Quarry.

Down at the foot of the Den, turn left on to Forest Road and then swing left again up Rubislaw Den North. The name of No. 13 – Glenburnie Park – is a reminder of the old distillery, and up at the top of the street is Rubislaw Den House, now a Nursing Home.

W.A. Brogden, author of an architectural guide to Aberdeen, called it "spooky Rubislaw Den House . . . all bays, towers, turrets and pointed windows". He added that it "somehow doesn't quite make it to Transylvania". It stands in beautiful grounds, and not everyone will see it as a spooky place – except, perhaps, after dark!

A number of houses at this end of the north Den were designed by William Kelly, and he himself lived at No. 62. Turn right into Moray Place and right again on to King's Gate. There are more towers and turrets as you go down this street, but the best-known building is the Atholl Hotel at No. 54. Brogden said that a wing built in 1880 "looks for all the world like a dry-run for Marischal College".

The last turn is right into Fountainhall Road, which is actually misnamed – it was originally Fountain Haugh. The "fountain" comes from six cisterns or fountain-houses which were built in 1766 along the old Fountainhall Road. The last fountain-house was rebuilt at the Duthie Park in 1903 (see Walk 8).

So it's down Fountainhall and back to Queen's Cross, where two churches – Rubislaw Church and Queen's Cross Church, designed by John Pirie – dominate the scene and Queen Victoria keeps an eye on the "granite grandery" of Aberdeen's West End.

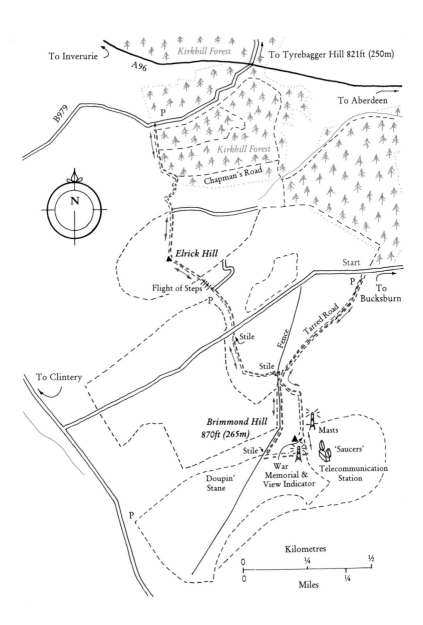

BRIMMOND AND ELRICK HILL

Brimmond Hill lies on the outer marches of Aberdeen, in the north-west corner of the city. It was from here that watchmen once kept an eye open for a beacon flaring on distant Castlehill, so that their link in the chain could be set alight when invasion was threatened. Now the "invaders" are walkers and bikers and Brimmond has become a link in another kind of chain – the Four Hills Country Walk.

The Four Hills Walk is a partnership between Aberdeen District Council, the Scottish Agricultural College and the Forestry Commission. At present it takes in Brimmond Hill (870 ft/265 m) and Elrick Hill, but there are plans to extend it to Tyrebagger Hill and the Hill of Marcus. This walk covers part of the Brimmond and Elrick section.

Start at the Brimmond Hill car park on the Bucksburn-Clinterty Road. From the car park a tarred road climbs up to the top of the hill, which is crowned by the huge masts and "saucers" of a telecommunication station. Away to the right is the familiar peak of Bennachie, with the sea to the left and the bustle of Aberdeen Airport behind you.

The road reaches a fork, the tarred section going left to the masts and a small path going uphill to a cairn on the summit. The right leg of the fork is a wider track going direct to the top. From here you can get a superb bird's eye view of the sea, the city and the surrounding countryside.

INFORMATION

Distance: 5 km (3 miles)

Start and finish: Brimmond Hill car park. To get there go by the Lang Stracht from North Anderson Drive to Kingswells, turn right to Newhills until you reach a T-junction, then go left and right again, passing a cemetery. Continue until you reach a cross-roads and turn left. The car park is on your left along this road.

Terrain: Good tracks on Brimmond Hill. Steep climb up Elrick Hill. Path down Elrick Hill is narrow and requires care. Strong footwear recommended.

Transport: If you are dropped off by car at Brimmond Hill and want to end the walk at Kirkhill, arrangements should be made to pick you up at the Kirkhill car park, off the Tyrebagger. Alternatively, you can take a bus into town from the Tyrebagger. Times from Bluebird Buses, Guild Street, Aberdeen (Tel. 01224 212266).

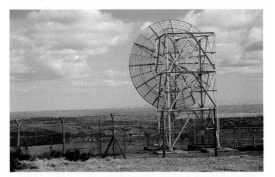

Mast on top of Tyrebagger.

On Brimmond walk.

One mast stands apart from the rest on Brimmond. Near it is a grassy picnic area, with seats and tables, and a short distance away, enclosed by a small dyke, is a curious metal structure which, surprisingly, turns out to be a memorial to the men of Newhills and district who gave their lives in the 1914–18 war. Lift the heavy metal top and underneath it is a mountain view indicator.

Between the picnic area and the mast is a waymarker for walkers following the official route, and from here a track goes down the west side of the hill to a fence with a stile over it. From the stile other paths spin off to the west, one going to a car park near Wynford, but they are not included in this walk. Instead, go right along the fence by a path which joins a horsetrail coming down from the summit.

Together, they head towards the tarred road coming up from the car park. To the left, set back from the road, you will see a stile crossing a fence into a field. Once over the stile, make your way down the field to yet another stile, which takes you by stone steps on to the Bucksburn-Clinterty road. Across the road is a track leading to a car park at the foot of Elrick Hill.

Elrick is a small hill, but the climb to the top is fairly steep and unsuitable for infirm or elderly people. The first part of the climb is by a flight of steps, then a rough path to the top. You will see a marker post with yellow arrows pointing round the hill and a brown arrow pointing ahead, directly up the hill. Follow the brown arrow.

There are a number of picnic tables and seats on top, which is wooded. The path bends a little to the right and heads downhill through moorland towards the Forestry Commission's Kirkhill Forest. The forest, which spreads out both north and south of the Tyrebagger road, had its first plantings back in 1922 – Norway spruce, Scots pine, European and Japanese larches, and Douglas fir.

As you go down Elrick Hill you can see Tyrebagger Hill and the Tyrebagger road running west to

Blackburn and Kintore. An old Chapman's Road went over Brimmond Hill to the Tyrebagger and there is said to be a blocked-up cave in the woods where robbers hid after holding up travellers on the north road.

Old records carry frequent references to "the Chapman road" and to a march stone "in an myre at the north syde of the hill of Brimmond". There is a Chapman Ford in the Howe of Bucksburn, linked with George Davidson, a packman who could scarcely read or write and yet became a wealthy man. Records show that he "built the bridge of Bucksburn, two myles from Abd, in the highway to Kintor".

So, as you go down Elrick Hill and into Kirkhill Forest, you are walking in the footsteps of the chapmen who made their way north by this route.

The track, which is stony for much of the way, bears right by a marker post with yellow and brown indicators and you pass a seat which looks down on the woodland ahead. A wooden fence has been erected on a short stretch of the track where there is a drop on the right-hand side. Beyond it is a small picnic area with two tables.

From the picnic area, stone steps take you down to the next leg of the track and soon you come to two wooden bridges over burns with little water in them. Farther on another bridge crosses a dried-up burn and here you go left.

A blue marker points right – this is a small circular route from the Kirkhill car park and is not part of your walk. Going left, you will soon find yourself in the car park. From it a motor road runs up to the Tyrebagger dual carriageway.

Unless you have arranged to be picked up at Kirkhill you will have to return the way you came to get to your car at Brimmond. On the other hand, if you are still full of enthusiasm and energy, you may want to carry on and tackle the heights of Tyrebagger Hill (see Walk 11).

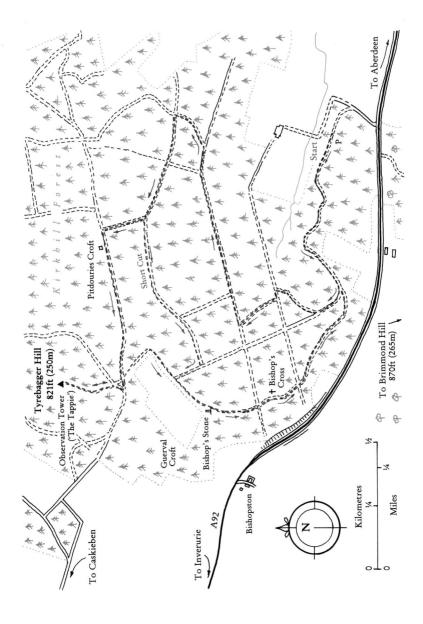

Tyrebagger Hill
821ft (250m)

Observation Tower
("The Tappie")

Kirkhill Forest

Pitdouries Croft

Short Cut

Guerval Croft

Bishop's Stone

Bishop's Cross

Start

P

To Aberdeen

To Brimmond Hill
870ft (265m)

To Caskieben

To Inverurie

A92

Bishopston

N

Kilometres
0   ¼   ½

Miles
0   ¼   ½

THE TYREBAGGER

This is a walk to the land of Waggles and Woggles. Most people know it as the Tyrebagger, a hill ridge forming a 7 km barrier across the route between the sea at Aberdeen and the inland country. When road-builders were trying to find a way through the ridge three centuries ago they were hampered by the boggy terrain – the "woggles" and "waggles".

"Woggle" is the old Scots word for a bog and "waggle" is a quaking bog. There was once a farm called Woggle in Kinellar and a Wagley in Newhills, and Boghead is still a familiar name in the area (see Walk 22). The name Tyrebagger itself is said to come from tir-bogaire, "land of the boggy place". Nowadays, a fast dual-carriageway carries traffic through the ridge.

At the end of the parking space, where the track starts, an information board sets out two forest walks – one, following white bands, 6 km (3¾ miles); the second, following white and orange bands, 4 km (2¾ miles). The shorter orange route covers part of the white route.

Our route is "white". Where it starts, a mountain bike trail runs alongside it for a short distance and then cuts off to the right. The main track continues, bending to the left, climbing gently. It passes a smaller track going off to the left and at this junction the first white/orange marker can be seen, pointing the way ahead.

For a short distance the countryside on the left is opened up, then the forest closes in as you head uphill, the climb becoming steeper. Stick to the main track. Further up you will see a wooden seat where the track goes right, with another white/orange post pointing this way. Ignore the narrow track to the left of the seat.

The track stretches away into the distance in a straight line. Another white/orange marker at a fork takes you left, climbing again.

INFORMATION

Distance: 7 km (4½ miles)

Start and finish: Tyrebagger car park. To get to the starting point drive up the A96 Aberdeen to Inverurie road until you are about 1¾ miles (3 km) past the roundabout leading to Aberdeen Airport. Turn right here, crossing the carriageway into a dead-end road where there is a sign saying "Forestry Commission – Kirkhill Forest". Then turn left into a large car park.

Terrain: Good tracks all the way, slightly rougher in parts on the return journey. Steepish climb on last lap to summit. Strong footwear recommended.

Public transport: A regular bus service passes the road from the Tyrebagger car park. Times from Bluebird Buses, Guild Street, Aberdeen (Tel: 01224 212266).

Refreshments: None en route. Take a flask for a drink on top of the hill.

Kirkhill Forest sign.

The route is well marked, but always keep an eye open for the white and orange marker posts. All the posts have white arrows on top of them indicating the route to follow. Here and there in the woods you will also see mountain bike posts and direction posts for orienteers.

Eventually, you come to a junction with a marker showing only an orange band and pointing to the left. This is the shortest "orange" walk. Your route, however, is to the right, following a "white" post. A few hundred metres farther on is a T-junction.

Another "white" post in the left-hand corner of the junction takes you left. The track passes a ruined cottage set back in the heather and in a further 400 m, you will see on the left a "white" marker pointing downhill – this is the alternative route back to the car park after you have climbed to the top of the hill.

Not far beyond the downhill arrow a path turns right up the hill – you are on the last lap of the outward walk. Another path from the Caskieben side of the Tyrebagger branches off the main track a little farther on and also goes up towards the summit, where the two paths meet.

A picnic table has been set up where the main track goes down to Caskieben, and from it you get a lovely view of the countryside, with Clachnaben's knotted head sticking up in the distance. But you will probably want to save your picnic for the top of the hill. The two paths run in tandem up the hill. It is a steep slope but not a long one. When the paths converge you can see the stone observation tower on the summit.

"Tappies" on Tyrebagger.

The stone tower, which has a flight of steps up to a circular viewing platform, guarded by railings, was built by a Dr William Henderson, of Caskieben. It is about 4 m high. The moorland on the west side of it has been cleared of trees so that a magnificent panoramic view greets visitors to what is known as the Tappie.

When the Tappie was built in the middle of last century, local folk held an annual Tappie Monday – the first Monday in May – when crowds flocked up the hill to celebrate Tyrebagger's answer to the Mither Tap. Sadly, so much damage was done to the tower that Tappie Monday was abandoned and when the Ordnance Survey revised the map of the district, they decided not to put the Tappie back in case the May ritual was revived.

On the way down from the summit go left down the main track and look for the marker post mentioned earlier. The path going right here starts off through thick woods and is fairly rough, but this is by far the more attractive half of the Tyrebagger walk.

View from Tyrebagger.

You will come to a sign on the right saying "Bishop's Stone". The stone is down through the trees beside a dyke at Gueval Croft, which can be seen in the background. It is an enormous stone, about 5 m long and 3 m wide. The initial M can be seen on it and two small, cup-shaped holes. The OS map shows a boundary stone at this point.

On the track downhill from the Bishop's Stone there is another link with the Bishop of Aberdeen – a huge cross of stone and turf laid out on the ground and said to mark the boundary of the Bishop's episcopal lands.

The track you are on eventually meets another major track and here your instinct tells you to go right, down the hill, drawn by the sound of traffic. In fact, your route lies to the left, uphill, as a white-orange marker indicates. Soon you join the main track from the car park. Go right here and you are soon back at the starting point.

The Tyrebagger Hill, 821 ft (250 m) high, offers a pleasant forest walk only a short distance from Aberdeen. The ascent is 450 ft (137 m) and the total distance is about 7 km.

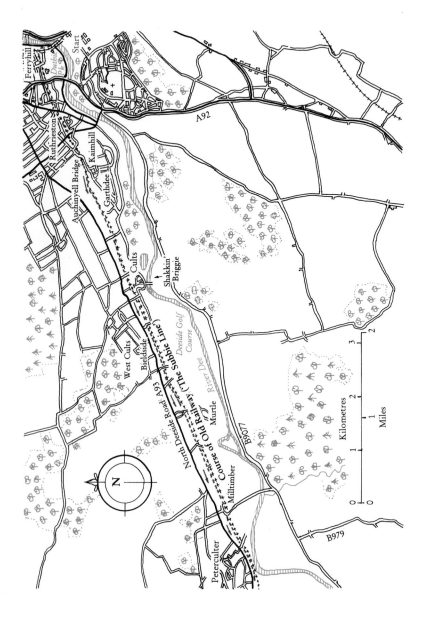

THE SUBBIE LINE

The Greek goddess of health, Hygeia, gives you a send-off when you walk the old Deeside railway line from Aberdeen's Duthie Park. She stands on top of a tall Corinthian column erected in 1898 in memory of Elizabeth Crombie Duthie, who gifted the land to the city to be used as a public park.

The park itself was opened in 1883, thirty years before the Duchess of Kent became the Deeside line's first Royal patron when she travelled by train from Banchory to Ferryhill Station. Queen Victoria followed two days later.

Hygeia's statue is only a short distance from the car park at the Polmuir Road entrance. Here, a few stone steps take you on to the Royal line ready for a healthy tramp to Culter, which was the terminus of the old Deeside suburban train service. On the left as you walk are the Winter Gardens, containing a wealth of tropical plants, sculptures and curios, while on the right are the back gardens of houses on Murray Terrace.

The first of many bridges on the line crosses the track at Great Southern Road, and a little further on you find yourself looking down into Holburn Street. Here, the bridge that carried trains over Holburn Street has been demolished, so you have to go down to street level by steps to get to the other side and back on to the line.

Holburn Street was an important station in the days of the "subbie" trains, disgorging to the West End of the city. It was also the station used by King Edward VII when he broke his holiday at Balmoral in 1906 and travelled from Ballater by train to open extensions to Marischal College at Aberdeen University.

Another bridge carries traffic over the line at South Anderson drive, then it is on past the platforms of Ruthrieston Station until you come to Auchinyell Bridge. Here, the walk begins to move away from the housing areas and out into open country.

INFORMATION

Distance: Culter one way 11 km (7 miles), Cults return 10 km (6 miles)

Start and finish: Car park in Duthie Park at Polmuir Road entrance.

Terrain: Good track all the way. No special footwear needed.

Public transport: Good bus service from Culter to Aberdeen. Details from Bluebird Buses, Guild Street, Aberdeen (Tel: 01224 212266), also from Tourist Information Office, St Nicholas House, Broad Street, Aberdeen (Tel: 01224 632727).

Refreshments: Hotels and cafes at Cults, Culter and elsewhere on North Deeside Road. Exits from rail track at a number of points.

The old line goes under a bridge over Pitfodels Station Road (there are steps up to the street) and a little further on are the platforms and the station building, converted for use as a private house. Beyond the Station the view opens out. Away on the left the Lower Deeside hills can be seen. Here, the old railway has become a tree-lined avenue and on the right are magnificent houses with beautiful gardens. This was where the city extended when the "subbie" trains operated – the start of the wealthy "stockbroker belt".

Then the station buildings of Cults loom up. Cults was one of the busiest suburban stations. Back in 1900, one writer commented on how new villas and cottages were turning it into "quite a large village". The clock on the platform has gone, but you can still see where it once ticked away the minutes as passengers – the first of what was to become an army of commuters – waited for the city-bound train. Outside, people park their cars on the station square, and if you want to "get off" at Cults you can walk up Station Road to the main street.

Beyond the station the line crosses a bridge over a steep brae coming down from Cults. Running parallel with it is a turbulent stream, tumbling through the Den of Cults towards the River Dee. From here you can see the river – and sticking up out of it the remains of the Shakkin' Briggie. Its official name was Morison's Bridge and at one time it was a vital link with folk living on the south side of the Dee, but, lacking proper maintenance, it finally gave way to the wind and weather.

The River Dee from the Subbie Line at Culter.

West Cults and Bieldside are next on the line, and on the left are the fairways of Deeside golf course, a popular private course in a lovely setting. Then comes a halt at Murtle, where a road goes up to the Waterwheel Inn. A big stone bridge with railings crosses a road to Murtle House, now occupied by the Rudolph Steiner School.

Birch trees line the track and in season broom and rhododendrons bring a bright splash of colour to the walkway. The next stop is Milltimber, where a road runs down from the A93 to the site of the old station. Milltimber was the nearest station to a well-known hostelry, the Mill Inn at Maryculter, which you can see from the track.

Not far from Milltimber a motor road links the North and South Deeside Roads, cutting across the old track. On the other side of the road, the fields and hills to the south open up as you enter the last lap of your walk.

As you approach Culter you go under what seems to be a bridge to nowhere, running into a field. The explanation is that at one time there was a farm on the right (north) side of the railway and the bridge was built so that the farmer could get his cattle over the Deeside line into pasture. The field goes down to the River Dee and for a short distance the track is quite close to it.

Pony riders use the Deeside track.

Finally, you "enter" Culter Station – and come to another bridge to nowhere. There are steps up to it and closer inspection shows that, as on the previous bridge, the road over it turned sharp right and went down the other side of the track to St Peter Church.

The name of the station is still clear on the long, wide platform. Culter was the terminus of the Deeside "subbie" service. The journey, covering 11 km, took 22 minutes on the "up" trip and 21 minutes on the "down". It is said that its service stood comparison with the London Underground.

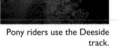
Sign at Culter Station.

To get back to the Duthie Park you have to retrace your steps along the line or return to town by a bus from the main street.

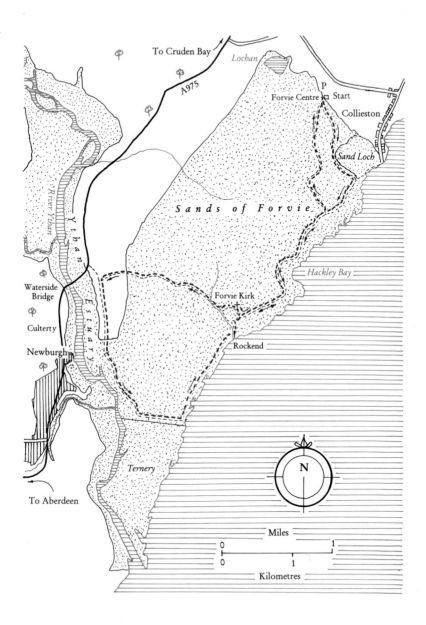

SANDS OF FORVIE

Yf evyr madenis malysone
Dyd licht upon drye land
Let nocht bee funde in Furvy's gleby's
Bot thystl, bent and sande.

That ancient curse comes to mind when you walk the "thystl, bente and sande" on the coastline between Collieston and Newburgh. It is said to have been brought down on the head of a Laird of Forvie who cast his three daughters adrift so that they would be denied their inheritance. But the curse turned out to be a blessing, for today Forvie has become one of Scotland's most important National Nature Reserves.

To explore "Furvy's gleby's" it is best to start at the Forvie Centre, a short distance off the road to Collieston, where Bob Davies, the Warden, presides over the fifth largest sand dune system in Britain. The Reserve was opened in January 1959, and is managed by Scottish Natural Heritage.

At the centre a sign points the way along a path leading into the Reserve. Away on the left you can see a row of old fishermen's cottages just outside Collieston. Watch for a marker post with arrows pointing ahead and to the left. Go left, towards the cottages.

Black-headed gulls squawk overhead as you come to the Sand Loch. Duckboard takes you round the head of the loch, where white bog-cotton serves as a reminder that the land here is marshy. The path comes out near a local football field, where there is a gate near the main coastal track from Collieston, the route you will follow. Here there is a large board with information – and a map – on Forvie, including the estuary, which is an optional extra on this walk.

Now you are heading along the clifftops. Herring gulls jostle for breeding sites on the cliffs, kittiwakes can be seen perched on precarious corners of the rocks, and fulmars, which make guttural growling noises and spit

INFORMATION

Distance: Rockend, 6.5 km (4 miles). Add 6.5 km (4 miles) for walk by estuary and ternery.
Start and finish: Forvie Centre. Take A92 road going north from Aberdeen, branching off on A975 to Newburgh. Cross River Ythan at Newburgh and continue 3 km to crossroads where the B9003 goes right to Collieston. Approaching the village, watch for sign to Forvie Centre on the right. Track runs up to the car park at centre.
Toilets: At Forvie Centre.
Terrain: Rough footpath along coast to Forvie Kirk. Care required on duckboard sections. On second leg up estuary there is a good path until branch-off point across sand dunes to the shore. Strong footwear recommended. Keep clear of the ternery. Some of the paths are suitable for wheelchair users.
Public transport: Bluebird Buchan Area Service 760–763. Information, Tel: (01224 212266).

Opening hours: *Forvie Centre,* Sat.-Sun. all year 1000–1700, Mon-Fri May-Aug. 1000–1700.
Worth seeing: Watch for eiders lying off coast and for breeding sea birds on rocks. Be careful – cliffs can be dangerous!

Warden at Forvie Nature Reserve.

foul-smelling oil at you, glide effortlessly along the cliff-tops.

Offshore, great rafts of eiders bob about on the water. They are the best-known birds at Forvie; not surprisingly, since some 5000 of them come to the area each summer. Those with the spectacular plumage are the males!

You pass a marker post, arrows pointing both ahead and back the way you came, while another arrow points right. The path to the right is your return route, so keep going straight ahead. The path dips down over wet marshland, duck-boarding carrying you over it and duckboard steps climbing up from it. The steps are steep, so you have to be reasonably fit.

The path narrows as you approach beautiful Hackley Bay, whose golden sands attract many picnickers.

Hackley Bay.

Here, duckboards go gently roller-coasting round the top of the bay, taking you over the awkward stretches. These and the steep steps going down to the bay are the work of the Warden and his enthusiastic volunteers.

From the north side of Hackley Bay you can see the great sweep of sand round to the Ythan estuary and beyond that to Balmedie and Aberdeen. Now you come to another marker post and turn right along a path that will take you to the remains of Forvie Kirk, built in the 12th century on the site of a chapel believed to date back to AD704.

This is all that remains of a settlement that was buried by the sand in the Middle Ages. In 1951, the foundations of a village of 19 circular huts 2000 years old were discovered under the sand. It was, say superstitious folk, all the results of the "madenis malysone", the curse uttered by the three daughters of the Laird of Forvie. At any rate, the "lost" village put the Sands of Forvie on the map.

From the ruined kirk a path takes you over a burn to a track running down to the Ythan estuary and to

Newburgh. If, however, you prefer to turn back at this point go left to the salmon fishing station at Rockend, a short distance along the main track.

Rockend is a nice spot to have your picnic, looking up along the bay to the mouth of the Ythan. It is also the point from which you start your return journey. First, however, let's look at the alternative . . .

Nets drying at Rockend.

When you leave Forvie Kirk go right along the track down to the Ythan and turn left along the estuary. Across the water is Newburgh, where the Culterty Field Centre, run by Aberdeen University's Zoology department, puts the birdlife of Buchan under the scientist's microscope.

Four species of tern breed among the sand dunes at the south end of the estuary. The most numerous is the Sandwich tern; there is a breeding colony of up to 1500 pairs in the ternery. There is also a colony of up to 50 pairs of little tern, one of Britain's rarest breeding seabirds. The elegant flight and spectacular diving of the terns can be seen as you walk up the estuary, where they feed on sand eels and other small fish.

The ternery is cordoned off during the breeding season between April and August. You cut left across the neck of the peninsula to the beach. The route is easily followed and once on the beach you make your way down the sands to Rockend.

From Rockend you make your way back to the Forvie Centre, passing the path which went off to Forvie Kirk. Watch out for a marker post pointing to the left, the alternative route back to the centre. This takes you past a small lochan which is a favourite haunt of ducks and gulls.

On your way back, keep an eye open for roe deer. There are more than a dozen on the Reserve. Other markers will lead you through the heathland to the Centre and your car.

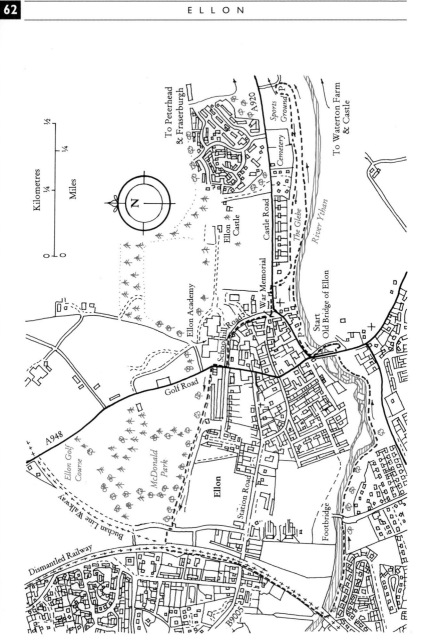

ELLON

Two bridges span the River Ythan at Ellon – one old, one new. In a way they are symbolic, for the "capital" of Buchan is a modern town that still has one foot in the past. The oil boom has turned it into a commuter-satellite of Aberdeen, but it retains its own distinctive character.

This walk starts in the shadow of Ellon's twin bridges – in the car park at Market Street, on the edge of the river. This was where the Moot Hill, now gone, once dominated the town, and where the Earls of Buchan held court and dispensed justice. The path in front of the car park, decorated with tall, elegant lamp posts, strikes out in both directions, clinging to the riverbank, but you go left, with back gardens and houses on one side and the river and open countryside on the other.

Not very far along the path you pass through a gate where a sign says, "Ythan Amenity Trust – The Glebe". The Glebe is a pleasant area of parkland, trim with trees and bushes, where you can sit and watch the river – and the world – go by. Just past the Glebe sign a short track goes up to Castle Road, the A920 to Peterhead and Fraserburgh. This is where you leave the park a little later.

The path through the Glebe takes you to a point where a narrower path goes off to the right and the main path goes left to another Castle Road exit. Stick to the narrow, right-hand path, which crosses a wooden bridge over a dried-up burn and heads towards Ellon cemetery. Keep going right by paths that take you to the riverside.

The Glebe Sports Ground can be seen ahead, with steps leading up to it, but before you come to it, turn left into a neatly laid-out car park. The road into the car park comes down from Castle Road, while another "dead-end" road – Meadow Way – leads to a housing estate on the Meadows.

INFORMATION

Distance: 5 km (3 miles).

Start and finish: Market Street car park, Ellon (over the bridge and turn right at roundabout). Ellon is 24 km (15 miles) north of Aberdeen on the A92.

Toilets: In Market Street car park.

Terrain: Good walking all the way on roads, paths and old Buchan railway line. No special footwear needed.

Refreshments: Ice-cream "shoppie" across from car park. Good pubs and restaurants nearby.

Public transport: Bluebird Buchan Area Service 760–763. Information, Tel: (01224 212266).

Old and new bridges over Ythan at Ellon.

When you walk on the banks of the Ythan you can see fishermen casting their lines, but once they "fished" for something more profitable – pearls. The Ythan was famous for its pearls.

There are two choices awaiting you at the Glebe car park. You can go up to Castle Road and walk into town on the next leg of the walk, or – a bonnier alternative – you can retrace your steps through the Glebe, sticking to the higher path. There are three exit-entrances to the Glebe on Castle Road, but it is best to go back to the gate where you entered and leave the park there.

Head for the war memorial, which is about 200 yards down Castle Road. Bear right by an old drinking trough where there is an inscription, "For the refreshment of weary beasts".

Turn sharp right up Schoolhill Road, passing Ellon Academy, which stands in a setting of trees and grassland. Turn right again up Golf Road and cross at the pedestrian lights. Beside the crossing is the entrance to the McDonald Park.

The long, tree-lined avenue through the park runs alongside Ellon golf course, but a little way up a stone obelisk in the middle of the track bars the way. An inscription on it reads, "This park was presented to the burgh of Ellon in 1928 by James Gordon McDonald of Rhodesia who lived within sight of this monument for over sixty years".

It is a lovely walk, passing a small rockery (with seats) presented to the town, but it looks as if they made a habit of putting up obstacles on the avenue, for farther on a huge stone blocks the way. McDonald of Rhodesia has been at it again. He had the stone put there to mark the Coronation of George VI and Queen Elizabeth (now the Queen Mother) in May 1937.

The avenue ends and you leave the park and turn right past a council depot. On the other side of the road, next to another golf course fairway, you will see a building with a sign "Ellon and District's Racquets Club". Cross the street here and you will see wooden steps leading to a dusty track on the edge of a housing estate. You are now on the Buchan Line Walkway.

Follow the Walkway until it goes down to the right and decants you on to a street near Station Road. Turn left and then left again on Station Road and the continuation of the Walkway can be seen on the opposite side of the street, marked by a wooden fence and a gate.

Ellon from railway bridge over Ythan.

Climb up on to the Walkway and you get a train driver's view of the Buchan countryside. Marathon walkers who decide to carry on will end up in Dyce. Not far ahead is a railway bridge over the Ythan. From it you can see a wooden pedestrian bridge downstream, linking the north and south banks of the river.

There are steps down to the riverbank at both ends of the bridge. Skip the first steps. Those at the far end of the bridge are rough and fairly steep, so be careful. They take you on to a tarmac path running alongside the river, which is fringed with a variety of trees including gean, sycamore, fir and alder.

You can cross the pedestrian bridge and go back to the car park on the north bank, but much more satisfying is the route by the south bank. The path winds its way through attractive parkland and then bears left to the riverside.

Before reaching the twin bridges, you can leave the path by steps going up to the Mercury Hotel. Otherwise, it's under the "new" bridge, with the roar of traffic above you, and a climb up a steep slope to the old bridge. The Auld Brig, as it is affectionately known, was built in 1793 and is a Category A listed building.

It looks good for another couple of centuries. No traffic here; only human feet cross its ancient surface. Out past the bollards at the north end and you are in busy Ellon again, only a few steps away from your car.

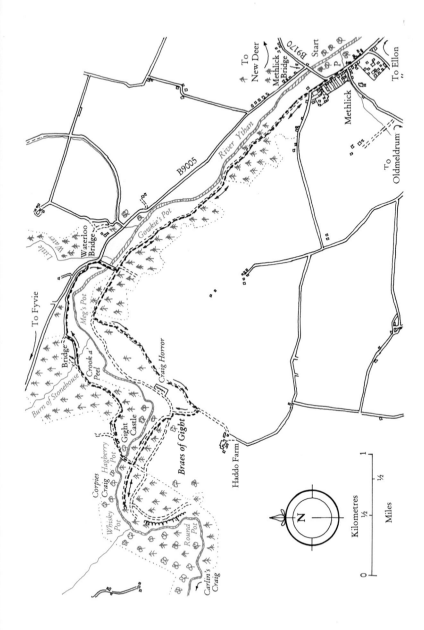

THE BRAES O'GIGHT

The Braes of Gight provide the setting for this outing . . . a walk through lovely countryside where the poet Byron's ancestors had their home. Here, you can walk in the footsteps of the "wild Gordons" and look at the gaunt ruins of the castle where they lived.

The walk starts in the village of Methlick, where you can leave your car in a car park off the main street. When you set off turn right from the car park and go along the main street until it swings right towards the River Ythan. Your way lies straight ahead, so cross the street to where a cobbled area at the junction is decorated with an old millstone.

Keeping left of the millstone, take the road past the public hall (built 1908), leaving it a little farther on to follow a track going through a builder's yard into the woods. There is a wire barrier across it to keep cars out.

Beech trees line one side of the track, but on your left the hill is bare. All along this walk you will see signs of massive tree-felling. The sound of gunfire can sometimes be heard, but no one is hunting the roe deer that can often be seen in the forest. The shots are from the Kingscliff Shooting Lodge, across the river, where clay pigeon shooting ranges are laid out.

When you come to a fork in the track the right-hand leg goes down to the Waterloo Bridge, an impressive name for a wee brig in a back-of-beyond spot in Buchan. It leads to the Methlick-Fyvie road (B9005). Near the bridge a stream called the Little Water runs into the Ythan. It is also known as the Black Water of Gight and there is a spot on the river called the Black Stank. Stank is a Scots word for a pool.

The Ythan throws up a number of curious place-names as you follow its course; downstream from the Waterloo Bridge is the Gowkie's Pot, while upstream is Meg's Pot. A gowk is a cuckoo and a pot is a pool.

INFORMATION

Distance: 9.5 km (6 miles).

Start and finish: Main Street car park in Methlick. Take the A92 from Aberdeen to Ellon and the B2005 from Ellon to Methlick. The village is about 13 km (8 miles) north-west of Ellon.

Toilets: In car park.

Terrain: Good track for much of the way, but short final leg of outward walk is rougher and less easy to follow. Steep climb up to Gight Castle from the Ythan. The Castle can be approached by a shorter and more direct route from parking area near the Waterloo Bridge. Strong footwear recommended.

Refreshments: Shops and pubs in village.

Public transport: Bluebird East Gordon Timetable, Service 290–291 to Methlick. Information, Tel: (01224 212266).

Footbridge below Gight
Castle.

Your route is not over Waterloo Bridge (you return by
it later), but straight ahead by the left fork. There are a
number of gates on the walk and after going through
the second one the track moves away from the river
and climbs gently uphill.

Soon you come to a second fork. Ignore the left leg,
which leads to Haddo Farm. Instead, go straight ahead
through another gate, which opens into a field where
cattle may be grazing, and follow the track as it runs
along the edge of a wood towards a fourth gate.
Remember to shut all gates behind you.

Behind the fourth gate a path cuts through thickly-
wooded Forestry Commission land. This short final leg
of the outward walk is rougher and less easy to follow.
About 100 metres from the gate look for a path going
through the trees on the right. It is usually marked by a
couple of bows tied to branches at the entrance, and it
is a short cut to a wooden bridge over the Ythan.

The alternative is to go a bit farther on to where the
track gets nearer to the river – you get glimpses of it
through the trees. When you come to a wide open
space at the end of the tree-line you have reached the
turning point of the walk. There is a huge rock face on
your left. Here, you should keep an eye open for a

group of young birch trees. Opposite these birches is
an opening in the wood which takes you to the river,
about 20 metres away.

The route now does a U-turn and follows the Ythan
downstream, running parallel with the outward track.
It is rough in places, but stick close to the river and
you can't go wrong. You pass the remains of a metal
bridge, but don't try to cross it; instead, continue along
the riverside until you reach the wooden bridge
mentioned earlier.

High above the river in this picturesque spot you will
get your first glimpse of Gight Castle, its gaunt ruins
perched almost on the edge of a deep drop to the river.
After crossing the bridge a narrow path takes you to
the top. It is a steep climb, but well worth the effort,
for wild flowers bloom on the brae and on your way up
you will have a magnificent bird's eye view of the
countryside, with the Ythan winding its way through
the valley below. The forestlands stretching into the
distance seem to mock the old taunt about "treeless
Buchan". Dr John B. Pratt, in his classic book *Buchan*,
described this corner of the Ythan valley as
"remarkable for its beauty and luxuriance".

On top of the path, where a stile takes you over a
fence to the castle, there is a Scottish Wildlife Trust
notice welcoming you to Gight Woods. The Trust
bought part of the Gight lands and the notice tells you
of their plans to plant more young trees, using natural
species such as wild cherry, oak and ash.

From the path you can see the Prop of Ythsie, a lofty
tower which dominates the countryside between
Pitmedden and Haddo House. It was built in memory
of George Gordon, 4th Earl of Aberdeen, who was
Prime Minister from 1852 to 1855.

The Gordons who lived in Gight Castle also won a
place in the history books, but for different reasons.
Sitting above the Ythan, under the ruins of this grim
Catholic stronghold, you will probably ask yourselves
the same question that was put in a verse by the

famous seer, Thomas the Rhymer:

> Twa men sat down on Ythan brae
> The ane did to the ither say,
> "An' what sic men may the Gordons o' Gight
>   hae been?"

The answer is that they were violent, lawless men. They were known as the wild Gordons of Gight and their dynasty was "crowded with murder and sudden death". Thomas the Rhymer also wrote a prophetic couplet:

> When the herons leave the tree,
> The lairds o' Gight shall landless be.

That prophecy came true in the time of Catherine Gordon, the mother of the poet Byron. Catherine was the unlucky 13th in this tragic line. Her husband – the poet's father – was Mad Jack Byron, who gambled away the family fortunes. When she used the last of her money to pay her husband's debts, the herons deserted Gight and crossed the Ythan to settle on Lord Aberdeen's land.

The names that appear on a map of Gight add to its gloomy image . . . Craig Horror, which is said to be a distortion of some older name; Crook a' Peel; Corpie's Craig and Carlins' (witches) Craig, the Round Pot and the Whisky Pot.

Down below the castle there is another "pot" in the Ythan with an unsavoury reputation – Hagberry Pot. There is a story about how one of the Lairds of Gight hid his treasure in this pot or pool and when he ordered a servant to go down for it the man refused because he thought the Devil was at the bottom.

In fact, the name of the pool is innocent enough for hagberry is a tree called the bird cherry, which can be seen growing on the Gight braes. Nor is it all gloom and doom in the Gight story. The annual Gight Games were held there a number of years ago and the highlight of the Games was the choosing of the bonniest lass to be the Rose of Gight for a year.

Gight Castle.

Gight Castle was built about 1560 by the second Gordon laird. It must have been a mighty stronghold, but it is a sad sight now. Outside it a notice warns that the structure is dangerous.

There is an intriguing little stone beside a wall of the castle. It can be seen when you climb up from the bridge. The inscription on it read "Lady Sneddon, Oct 81 to April 94", but there is nothing to show whose pet dog is buried in the shadow of the old castle.

Look for another stone – an old milestone – near the castle. The faded inscription on it reads "HH 5" – Haddo House 5 miles. From here, follow a track leading to a gate which will put you on the road back to Methlick. It runs through lovely woodland until you come to a bridge over the Burn of Stonehouse.

A short distance beyond the bridge the track runs up to the main Fyvie road, cutting through another denuded hill, but your way is to the right, following the Ythan. Across the river you will see the track you started out on, with the first of the devastated treeless hills behind it.

Soon you will see the Waterloo Bridge ahead. The track runs on to join the Fyvie road near the bridge, but before you come to it you will pass a small car park on the left. This is used by fishermen, but weekend walkers also park there on their way to Gight Castle. For those who want a direct route to Gight, without going up the west side of the Ythan, this is a good place to start.

When you reach the Methlick-Fyvie road turn right over the Waterloo Bridge, then left, and soon you are back in the village.

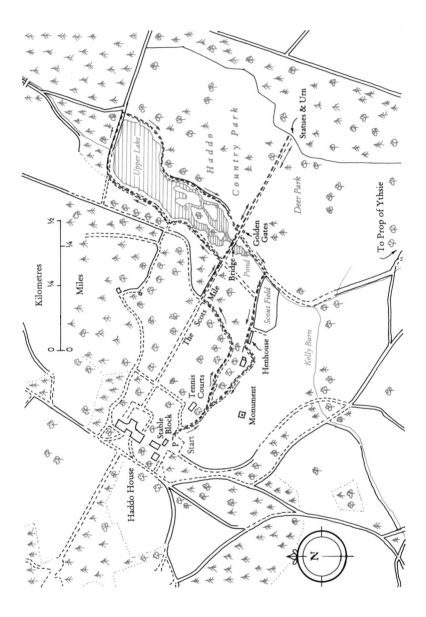

Haddo House

Stable Block

Tennis Courts

Start

Monument

Henhouse

Scout Field

Bridge

Pond

Golden Gates

Upper Lake

Haddo Country Park

Deer Park

Statues & Urn

The Scots Mile

Kelly Burn

To Prop of Ythsie

Kilometres

½ ¼ ¼ 0

Miles

HADDO

Wh…hen you wander through Haddo Country Park you are walking in the footsteps of a host of famous people . . . Queen Victoria, Gladstone and Lord Rosebery; Sir George Otto Trevelyan, the historian and biographer; George du Maurier, the novelist, and many more.

The country park came into being in 1978, when Haddo House and its garden were transferred to the care of the National Trust for Scotland. At the same time, 180 acres of land were given to Grampian Regional Council to establish a park. Today, it is a magnet for hundreds of visitors.

The start of this walk is the large parking area in front of the stable block at Haddo. Before you set off, look for an information board at one end of the parking area. It carries a big map of the country park. To the right of it a few stone steps lead up to a path which curves round to the right. This is the start of your walk.

On your right as you set off is a tall obelisk built by George Gordon, 4th Earl of Aberdeen, in memory of his brother Arthur, who was killed at Waterloo. The monument is not, in fact, in the country park, but a path from the car park leads to it.

The trees bend their branches in salute as you go through the woods. If you tried to name them all you would have your work cut out, for there are 70 species

Haddo House.

INFORMATION

Distance: 5 km (3 miles)

Start and finish: Haddo Country Park. There is a large parking area near Haddo House. To get to Haddo House take the A92 north from Aberdeen, branching off at Murcar on the B999 to Pitmedden and Tarves. Before reaching Tarves look for National Trust for Scotland signs directing you to Haddo House.

Terrain: Good walking all the way. Strong footwear recommended in wet conditions.

Toilets: Stable block at Haddo House.

Refreshments: Tea room in Stable block, also souvenir shop.

Public transport: Bluebird buses run direct to Haddo. Information, Tel: (01224 212266). Car advised.

Opening hours: *Haddo House:* Easter weekend, 1 May-30 Jun, 1 Sep-30 Sep, daily 1330–1730. 1 Jul-31 Aug daily 1100–1730, 1 Oct-22 Oct, Sat-Sun only 1330–1730. Last admission 1645. Admission charge. *Haddo Country Park:* Open all year, daily 0930-sunset.

of trees and shrubs in the park, from a horse chestnut – the familiar "conkers" tree – near the Stables Block to mighty beeches and aspen which have grown at Haddo for hundreds of years. There are wooden signs identifying the trees.

The short path from the car park joins one of the main surfaced roads from the stables block. Follow the blue arrow and when you come to a fork leave the surfaced road and go left, through an area where jackdaws nest in the spring. Through the trees on the right is a red-brick building. Have a guess at what it is – you'll find the answer on the way back!

Soon you are at a cross-roads. Here, on your left, a long avenue runs down from Haddo House, while on the right it stretches away to the Deer Park. This avenue is known as the Scots Mile. There are actually two avenues, one being the Victoria Avenue planted to mark Queen Victoria's Jubilee, and together they measure a Scots mile – 1984 imperial yards (about 2 km). A "normal" mile is 1760 yards.

Deer statue in Deer Park at Haddo.

Go right at the cross-roads. Ignore an arrow pointing left through the woods (you come back to that later) and follow a blue arrow pointing ahead to a bridge over the Kelly Burn – and to the Golden Gates. This is the name given to magnificent black and gold gates carrying the Gordon coat of arms.

On each side of the Golden Gates is a deer dyke enclosing the Deer Park, which dates back to 1690. The dyke once penned in a herd of fallow deer, and there are two statues of fallow deer at the top of the Deer Park. The fallow deer have long since gone (they were replaced by Highland cattle in 1898), but if you are lucky you may see wild roe deer coming out of the woods.

A wide grassy avenue climbs up to the statues and the end of the Scots mile. Beyond the statues is a huge urn perched on an equally massive pedestal. It was erected by George Gordon, 4th Earl of Aberdeen, in memory of his first wife. The 4th Earl was Prime Minister of Great Britain from 1852 to 1855. He was a poor Prime Minister but a good laird, for at Haddo he brought a neglected estate back to life, planting fourteen million trees before he died.

From the top of the Deer Park you get an impressive view down the Scots mile to the Victoria Avenue and Haddo House. Make your way back to the Golden Gates. After going through the gates, ignore for the moment a blue arrow pointing left. Instead, continue over the Kelly Burn bridge. There is a pond on either side of the bridge and scores of mallard duck can be seen there. They will come waddling out of the water for titbits. "They come out and mug you," jokes David Patterson, the park ranger.

Go along the avenue until you come to the blue arrow pointing right. This takes you on a lovely walk through a small woodland on the edge of the lake, passing a number of pools where frogs and toads spawn. Their numbers are apparently declining – at one time there were notices warning people that there were frogs crossing.

The path takes you on to a wide track which, as you turn right, runs up the side of the Upper Lake, opening out to give you a good view over the water. Watch for a sign on the right indicating a path to a bird hide. Reaching a T-junction you go right and round the head of the lake, where a wooden platform with a fence juts out into the water. Here, swans will come to the platform to be fed. There is a lifebelt in case you fall in!

The track curves round the top of the lake and, turning back, crosses a wooden bridge over the Burn of

Kelly. Beyond the bridge you go parallel to the lake, sticking fairly close to a fence on the right. After passing another bird hide you reach the Golden Gates and pass through them for the third time.

Now go left where you earlier saw the blue arrow directing you along the side of the deer dyke. Cross the burn by another small wooden bridge and you will see a post pointing left to a path cut through an area of rough grass. Where the rough grass gives way to a mown field, another post points in the direction of a gate and trees on the far side of the field.

As you cross the field you will see away to the right the red brick building you passed at the start of the walk. You will come to a path which runs down to steps leading up to the front of the building. Have you guessed what it is? On one of the doors there is a sign, "The Old Pheasantry", and it is known as the Pheasantry Building. There seems to be some doubt about whether or not it ever housed pheasants, although today the estate rears about 10,000 pheasants each year for shooting.

Incidentally, the wooden pheasant signs you see have nothing to do with the Pheasantry or with rearing pheasants. They mark the boundary between the Country Park and the estate, which carries on the business of farming, forestry and game.

But back to the Pheasantry. This stylish building was constructed in 1885 – as a Henhouse! That, at any rate, is what some people say and local folk actually speak about it as the Poultry Yard. According to a Ranger Service leaflet, the locals claim that "it never saw anything more glamorous than a Rhode Island Red". The rangers would love to know the true story.

Today, the Henhouse is used by local scouts and by the Park's Ranger Service, who work with schools, handicapped groups, senior citizens and other clubs. There are toilets in the building.

Leaving the Henhouse, follow the blue-arrow path back to the Stable Block and the car park. Note the tennis courts on the right – you can book a game there. There is also an adventure playground in the park.

Before you leave the Country Park it is worthwhile taking a look at Haddo House (see Information for times) and the garden laid out there when the famous house designed by William Adam, was built in 1732. It fell into disrepair, but in 1805 the 4th Earl renovated it with the artist and landscape gardener James Giles.

There is a final reminder of the 4th Earl's contribution to Haddo when you leave the estate. On the hill of Ythsie, between Haddo and Pitmedden, there is a tall stone monument known as the Prop of Ythsie. The word "prop" means a landmark, and this one was built as a memorial to the 4th Earl. It is well worth a visit. A small car park has been laid out on the approach to the monument. It is said, not without justification, that from here you get the best view in Buchan.

Haddo Country Park is a magical place. There are other walks to be followed and other things to see. A souvenir shop and a coffee room are available in the Stable Block.

The Henhouse.

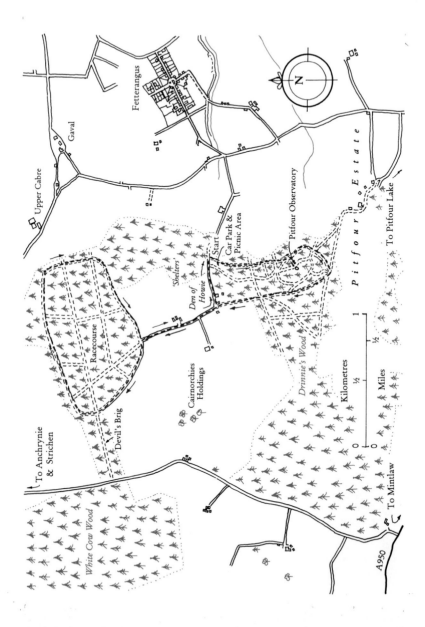

PITFOUR

I t's off to the races on this walk . . . to see where a north-east Laird once held his own Ascot in the heart of Buchan. From a tall tower in Drinnie's Wood, near Fetterangus, the Laird and his guests watched their horses galloping around a circular racecourse laid out in the high ground above Cairnorchies.

At Fetterangus, signposts point the way to a car park and a small but attractive picnic area a short distance west of the village. A sign tells you it was provided by Banff and Buchan District Council and Banff and Buchan Enterprise Trust in association with Forest Enterprise.

From the picnic area a track leads through a stretch of moorland to the Pitfour Observatory. Incidentally, you won't see any signs banning dogs from the tower, but just in case you're thinking about it the authorities have provided a dog hitching post near the entrance.

The Observatory, an octagonal, three-storey harled structure with a crenellated parapet, was built by the eccentric 5th Laird of Pitfour, Admiral George Ferguson, who died in 1867. It was purchased and restored by Banff and Buchan District Council in 1993 and opened in September of that year.

Inside the entrance, 17 wooden steps on the left lead to the first floor, but if you want to go higher take the metal stairs on the right – 49 steps – leading to the second floor. Here, a series of large windows open up an impressive panoramic view of Buchan.

Admiral Ferguson, who became Laird of Pitfour in 1821, did his best to outdo his predecessors. The Admiral, who was the illegitimate son of George Ferguson, 4th Laird of Pitfour, was (perhaps

INFORMATION

Distance: 5.5 km (3½ miles).

Start and finish: Picnic area near Fetterangus. To get there take the A92 Aberdeen-Fraserburgh road, via Ellon, to Mintlaw. Continue on A92 and about 2 km north of Mintlaw turn left to Fetterangus. There are signs pointing the way to the car park and picnic area near Pitfour Observatory.

Terrain: Good walking on roads and tracks. No special footwear needed.

Toilets: Fetterangus.

Refreshments: At Aden Country Park or in Mintlaw.

Public transport: Car necessary.

Path to Observatory from car park.

surprisingly for a naval man) always happiest on the back of a horse. He built great stables north of Pitfour House (now demolished), and opened a riding school. Then, in 1845, he built his racecourse.

Looking north from the Observatory, following the line of the track to the car park, you can see in the distance the high ground where the Admiral built the racetrack. One way to get to it when you leave the Observatory is to go down the entrance path and turn right on to the track from the car park. Go right again at the bottom of the brae, and then right once more a short distance farther on, with the Observatory still on your right. This track, running almost parallel with the car park track, has moorland on the right and open fields on the left.

You pass a disused red-brick farm building on the left, negotiating an old gate, and a little way ahead come to a cottage with neat, well-kept gardens and lawns. The area around the cottage is decorated with old ploughs and other farm implements.

The road going right from the cottage leads back to the car park. You go this way on the return leg of the walk, but for the present carry straight on towards a farm on the right.

A minor road on the left also leads to a farm – Cairnorchies. The racecourse lies in the centre of five points on the map, Cairnorchies being one of them. The others are White Cow, Auchrynie, Cabre and Gaval.

Leaving the farm behind, you come to a point where the track you are on bears left and a rougher, narrower track comes in from the woods on the right to join it. The tracks merge and become one, which is what they were last century, for you are now on part of the old racecourse.

It is more than likely that this was where the races started and finished, for it was well within sight of the Observatory, although the Admiral would have needed his telescope to see which horse was first past the post. The tower is about half a mile from the race-course; why it was built so far away is anybody's guess. It may have been because it was nearer Pitfour House.

As you walk on, look back and you will see the tower in the distance. Maybe the ghost of the old Laird is sitting on top of it watching you through his telescope, or maybe the Devil himself is there. A track on your left runs down to a bridge shown in an 1870 map as the Devil's Brig. This track leads to the Mintlaw-Strichen road and the White Cow Wood, where there are picnic areas and forest walks.

The racecourse curves to the right. Across farmlands on the left, Mormond Hill and its once warlike communication masts can be seen. The moor on the right is heavily planted with young trees.

Eventually, you pass another track going off to the left. This winds away to the Den of Howie and pitches you out on to the Fetterangus road almost opposite the car park. Your way, however, is still straight ahead, young trees giving way to old woodland.

When the trees on the left end, look across the fields and you will see the Pitfour Observatory poking up above the horizon. Now you have almost come full circle, back at the point where the track from the cottage meets the track from the woods.

Turn left and head down past the Cairnorchies road to the cottage, where you turn left again and go up the Fetterangus road to the picnic area and the car park. Just before you reach it you will see on the left a gate across the track where the detour from the racecourse comes to an end.

Pitfour Observatory.

The 1870 map shows a circular area in the Den of Howie near the track marked "Shelters". What the "Shelters" were seems to be a bit of a mystery. Shelters for the horses? Shelter for the Laird and his guests? Who knows! At any rate, it is here that we take our leave of the Admiral, one of the most picturesque figures of the last century in Buchan, and of the corner of Buchan that became the Ascot of the North.

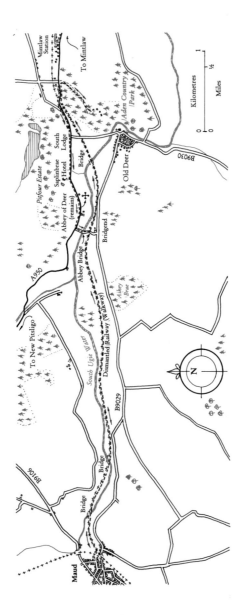

MAUD TO ADEN

When the railway came to Buchan in 1866 the little village of Maud was suddenly put on the map. It became an important railway junction for lines branching north and east to Fraserburgh and Peterhead. It also helped the village to become a market centre for Buchan cattle. Today, by comparison, the cattle trade is minimal – and the railway has gone.

But you can still go down the Buchan line – on foot. The Buchan Countryside Group, with the help of other organisations, has opened up the line as a Walkway. This walk takes you along a section of the old railway from Maud to Mintlaw, ending at Aden Country Park, which has been described as "a haven for people and wildlife".

The railway offices on the platform have been divided into work units for local businesses, while an attractive parking and picnic area has been laid out behind the station. From the station follow one of the paths down to the Maud-Old Deer road (B9029). Cross the road and a little way down you will see steps leading up to the Walkway.

The path is narrow at the start, hemmed in by broom bushes, briar roses, bluebells, marguerites and other wild flowers. Yellow buttercups make a golden path of the old line. On this first stretch, it is hard to believe that trains once came puffing up the track.

You cross a minor road going down to sewage works and farther on go over a rusty bridge spanning the South Ugie Water. There are occasional reminders of the railway days . . . numbered signs, a faded notice board at a farm crossing, a deserted linesman's hut.

If you are walking on the Walkway in early July you will see on your right caravans and tents standing on a gently-sloping hill overlooking the Ugie – they are there for the Aikey Fair. This was said to be the greatest horse fair in the north-east of Scotland, but

INFORMATION

Distance: 11 km (7 miles).

Start and finish: Maud Station. From Aberdeen take the A92 to Ellon and follow the A948 north, branching off by the B9106 to Maud.

Terrain: Narrow footpath at start, widens to old railway track. Part of return walk on A950 New Pitsligo-Mintlaw road – take care. No special footwear needed.

Toilets: At Aden Country Park.

Refreshments: Cafe/restaurant at Aden Country Park.

Public transport: Bluebird East Gordon Timetable, Service 251. Information, Tel: (01224 212266).

Opening hours: *Aden Country Park: All year round, daily, sunrise – sunset. Heritage Centre, May-Sept. daily 1100–1700. Hareshowe Farm, as Heritage Centre. Wildlife Centre, May-Sept. weekend only 1400–1700. Caravan and camping site, Apr.-Sept.*

the horses have long since gone from Aikey Brae, or most of them, and what you see now on Aikey Sunday (usually the first after 19 July) is not much more than a glorified fairground.

But Aikey Brae has another claim to fame. It was there that the Battle of Aikey Brae was fought in 1308, when Edward Bruce, brother of Robert the Bruce, defeated the Comyn Earl of Buchan and wrought vengeance on the Comyn family with the herschip (harrying) of Buchan.

Less than a mile beyond Aikey Brae you can see on your left traffic on the road from New Pitsligo (A950) heading down past the Abbey of Deer on its way to Mintlaw. Road, river and rail track come together at Bridgend just before reaching the Abbey. There are actually two bridges here, a bridge over the railway track and the Abbey Bridge over the Ugie.

Abbey of Deer.

Bridgend takes its name from the Abbey Bridge – and a very odd brig it is! Drivers crossing it find to their amazement that one half of the bridge is narrower than the other. The thin half is on the north side of the bridge, the fat half on the south side.

The bridge marked the boundary between the estates of the Fergusons of Pitfour and the Russells of Aden and its present appearance stems from a feud between the two lairds. When the Fergusons built Pitfour Loch, the Russells said it would cause flooding in Aden. The Fergusons, however, went ahead with their loch-building, but the Laird of Aden got his revenge. When the Fergusons widened the bridge to allow coaches to pass over it, the Russells refused to widen their side. The result is a half-and-half bridge that should surely claim a place in the Guinness Book of Records.

The Fergusons had a reputation for eccentricity and no one deserved it more than Admiral George Ferguson, 5th Laird of Pitfour. The result of one of his brainwaves left its mark on the Abbey of Deer, which is a short distance from Bridgend. The Admiral decided in 1854 to build a Pitfour Mausoleum, but to do it he pulled down the walls of the Abbey and used the stones to put up what one writer called "nothing so much as a Heathen Temple".

The old Buchan line passes within a stone's throw of the Abbey walls and a little farther on you can see Saplinbrae House, now a hotel, off the New Pitsligo-Mintlaw road. Incidentally, you can also see sticking up behind the hotel the top of the Pitfour Observatory, another of the mad Admiral's crazy creations (see Walk 17).

This stretch of the walk is a wilderness of wildflowers, trees and bushes closing in on you, while the road from Maud is on the right almost at your elbow. Then it's out into the open and across another iron bridge over the South Ugie. The South Lodge of Pitfour estate can be seen on the left and, after passing a stretch of aspen trees, you are almost at the path taking you into Aden Country Park.

Aden, with its gutted mansion house, was the home of generations of the Russell family. Now it draws hundreds of visitors to Mintlaw. It boasts an award-winning Heritage Centre, where you can turn back the clock to life on the estate farm in the 1920s, and its restored farm buildings in the Round

Aden House.

Square include a Horseman's House where bannocks and oatcakes are baked for visitors. There is also a working farm, an adventure playground for the youngsters, a cafe-restaurant, a craftshop, and much more.

It is worth starting your return walk on the Mintlaw road so that you can visit the Abbey of Deer. The Abbey Bridge is only a short distance beyond it. After that, it's back on to the track and up the line to Buchan's once-great cattle town at Maud.

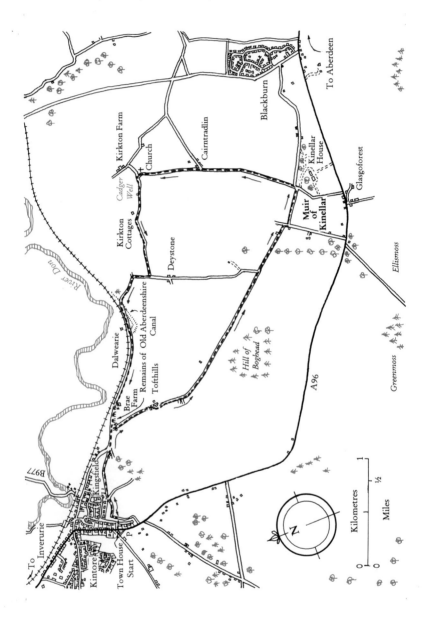

KINELLAR

A walk by the old Aberdeenshire Canal – or, at any rate, a small part of it – is included in this jaunt into a corner of the Garioch. It begins in the royal burgh of Kintore, where a small but handsome Town House, with curving forestairs and a clock tower, stands on an island site overlooking the busy main street.

The Town House, which dates from the early 18th century, is your starting point – there is a car park behind it. On the other side of the main street is the parish church. Cross the street and follow the church round into Kingfield Road, which goes east out of the village, past a sign to Deystone.

When the row of houses comes to an end, the road swings round towards the River Don. Look for a house on the right-hand side as it bends towards the river. Just beyond it is a high embankment, fringed with trees. Climb up its grassy slope and you are standing on the towpath of the old Aberdeenshire Canal, which ran between Port Elphinstone and Aberdeen nearly two centuries ago. Below, on the right, is the dried-up canal bed.

When you walk along the towpath look for the canal's 14th milestone at the edge of the path. It faces into the canal and away from what is now a motor road. Half-miles as well as miles were marked on some of the stones because journeys on the barges were charged by the half-mile. Eleven milestones can still be traced along the 30 km length of the canal.

Farther on you come to Brae Farm, where there is a break in the canal, which continues on the other side of the farm entrance. Turn right, past the farmhouse, and go up the brae that gives the farm its name. After this gentle climb the track drops down to another farm, Tofthill. It goes through the farm, turns sharp right and then left,

INFORMATION

Distance: 9.5 km (6 miles).

Start and finish: Car park at rear of Kintore Town House, Kintore, which is 20 km (12 miles) from Aberdeen, is reached by the A96 road to Inverness.

Terrain: Walking is on roads, canal path, and farm track. Strong footwear recommended.

Toilets: In Kintore main street near Town House.

Refreshments: In the village.

Public transport: Bluebird Coach Timetable, Service 10 to Kintore. Information, Tel: (01224 212266).

Kintore Town House.

Old canal path and milestone.

and pushes on to Kinellar. This was the old route from Kintore to Kinellar. Records show that before the "modern" Inverurie highway was built in 1800 the road from Kintore to the Muir of Kinellar was "in daily use".

Beyond Tofthill parts of it can be wet and muddy in bad weather. Six or seven centuries ago much of this countryside was marshland, as names like Hill of Boghead, Greenmoss and Ellismoss testify. From the track you get a striking view of the surrounding countryside. At one point you come to a fork. The right-hand leg goes down to the Inverurie road, but your way is to the left, where there are whins on either side of the track.

About 2 km from Tofthill you pass two houses, one called Mondeen, the other Haycorn House. From here the track goes on until it turns sharp right down a surfaced road that leads to Glasgoforest on the A96 Inverurie road.

About 100 m along the surfaced road turn left up a wide, rough track, part of which is fringed on the right by a small beech wood. This is shown in some maps as the Muir of Kinellar, but today the "muir" is under cultivation. If you prefer it, you can get off the track and make your way along a narrow path in the wood. The road is a fairly short one and ends in a T-junction. A short distance to the right is a rear entrance to Kinellar House.

Your way, however, is to the left at the T-junction, following a road that will eventually take you back to Kintore. The road is quiet, but keep an eye open for traffic. After turning left, you pass a side road to Blackburn. Beyond it is an imposing house called Carnmhor, with an ornate garden fence and a big sun parlour. Its front windows command a magnificent panoramic view. Farther on is a large farm – Cairntradlin – a name associated with the well-known Sylvester Campbell farming family.

Ahead lies the parish church, tucked away in remote farmland about 2 km north of Blackburn. The manse is on the left, a tall, stately building that tends to dwarf the wee kirk. Over the garden gate are the initials J. W. and the date 1615. "J. W." was the Reverend John White, who was preaching at Kinellar Church when the kirk bell that hangs there today was ringing out nearly three centuries ago.

The old kirk seems curiously isolated from its parishioners. It is quiet and peaceful, and as you look out over the spreading fields to Bennachie and the distant hills, the words inscribed on one of the tombstones are brought to mind. It reads: "Heart, if you've a sorrow, take it to the hills". A nice sentiment.

The road past the church goes right to Kirkton Farm, but you go left, down past Kirkton Cottages and a sign saying "Deystone Clydesdales".

A "horsey" greeting on the walk.

Road, rail and river – and the old canal – all come together about 800 m from Kirkton Cottages. The path of the canal can be seen across the fields on the left. On the right is Dalwearie, which was a horse-changing station when the barges ran. They were pulled by two or three horses in tandem, with a boy riding on the first horse.

The starting point of the canal was at Port Elphinstone, on the outskirts of Inverurie, 5 km north of Kintore. It was from "The Port", as it was called locally, that the *Countess of Kintore* set off on its inaugural run in 1807. Flags flew, bands played, and a gun on the barge boomed out in celebration.

Less than half a century later the dream seeped into the silt and mud of the canal as it was drained to make way for the Great North of Scotland Railway. Now it is only a memory, but as you make your way along the last lap of the walk, passing Brae Farm again and the 14th milestone, you can still find links with the great days when the "Passage Boat" sailed from "Inverury" to Aberdeen at 2.30 pm every day except Sunday.

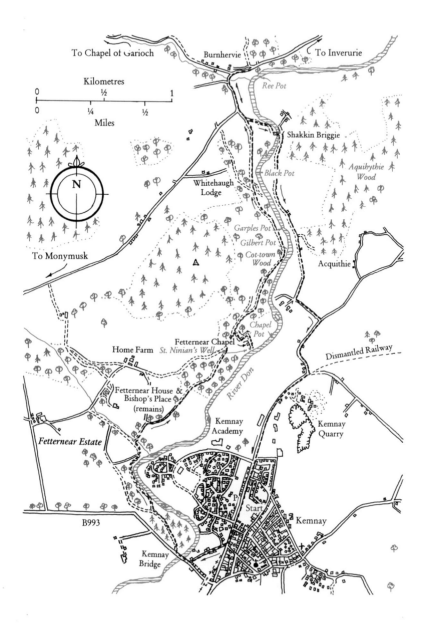

To Chapel of Garioch

Burnhervie

To Inverurie

Ree Pot

Kilometres
0   ½   1
0   ¼   ½
Miles

Shakkin Briggie

Aquihythie
Wood

Black Pot

Whitehaugh
Lodge

N

Garples Pot

Gilbert Pot

Cot-town
Wood

To Monymusk

Acquithie

Chapel
Pot

Fetternear Chapel

Home Farm   St. Ninian's Well

Dismantled Railway

River Don

Fetternear House &
Bishop's Place
(remains)

Kemnay
Academy

Kemnay
Quarry

Fetternear Estate

B993

Kemnay
Bridge

Start

Kemnay

FETTERNEAR

An ancient estate where the Bishops of Aberdeen had a Summer Palace and a shooting lodge nearly eight centuries ago is the setting for this walk. It follows a path along the banks of the River Don from Kemnay Bridge to the Shakkin' Briggie and Burnhervie, passing near to the ruins of a great mansion house.

Leaving your car in the car park at Kemnay, turn right along Acquithie Road, then right again at the first opening. This takes you over an old railway bridge and down to Riverside Road where, taking another right-hand turn, you cross the Don by Kemnay Bridge. A short distance on is the entrance to the estate of Fetternear.

The imposing entrance gate carries two old signs saying that pedestrians are welcome except when the gates are closed, which is rarely. There is, in fact, a small pedestrian gate set into the main gate, and the estate has no objection to this being used if the gates are shut.

Beyond the gate, passing a lodge on the left, the track heads through the Fetternear woods, sticking fairly close to the River Don at first. Across the river is a modern housing estate. Soon, track and river part company, the track bending away to the left.

Farther on, a rather dilapidated bridge crosses a burn

INFORMATION

Distance: 9.5 km (6 miles).

Start and finish: Car park in Acquithie Road, Kemnay. From there go right and follow road to bridge over River Don at entrance to Fetternear estate. Kemnay, which is 22 km (14 miles) west of Aberdeen, is reached by taking the A96 and branching left along the B994.

Terrain: Good paths all the way; no special footwear needed. If returning by road there is a steep climb up from the Shakkin' Briggie to the road. Also, watch out for traffic on this route.

Toilets: In Kemnay.

Refreshments: In Kemnay.

Public transport: Bluebird West Gordon Timetable, Service 220 to Kemnay. Information, Tel: (01224 212266).

The Don from Fetternear path.

on the right, taking you on the first leg of a track towards the Don. Looking across the fields on the left you will see the ruins of the House of Fetternear, which succeeded the medieval Bishop's Palace. Practically nothing of the Palace remains.

The Palace, no longer being used as an episcopal residence, became uninhabitable in the middle of the 16th century, when the Barony came into the possession of the Leslies of Balquhain. William Leslie, 9th Baron Balquhain, built a new house, which was altered and improved by succeeding generations of Leslies. Over the years, it grew from a small tower house into a large mansion.

The end of the House of Fetternear came in December 1919, when a servant left a pan of hot ashes in a back store room and set fire to kindling, coals and oil. The mansion house was destroyed. Today, the house is a dangerous ruin, yet even seen from the distance its mellow sandstone walls retain some of its past glory. In the Proceedings of the Society of Antiquaries, 1970-71, H. Gordon Slade wrote: "It deserves to survive as an unusually interesting example of the transformation of a Laird's Tower into a Nobleman's Palace and thence into a Gentleman's Seat".

Continuing on the walk, you come to a fork, where a notice on a tree says "Fishing", with an arrow pointing to the right. This is your route, following the track on the line of the river. Across the Don is Kemnay Quarry, where silver-grey stone from the Hill of Paradise helped in the building of such national landmarks as the Holborn Viaduct in London, the Thames Embankment and the Forth Railway Bridge. Kemnay Academy can be seen near the quarry.

Going through a gate, you come to a huge green corrugated barn on the right which has seen better days. A little farther on, a road cuts back to the Home Farm and the ruined mansion house. Do NOT go this way – continue on the main track and you will see a rough path going right to the river. Here there is another tree sign, this one pointing to the "Chapel

Pool". This is shown on the map as Chapel Pot. A pot
is a deep pool and there are a number of "Pots" on this
stretch of the Don, among them Gilbert Pot and the
Black Pot. North of the Chapel Pot, between Cot-
town Wood and Acquithie Wood (pronounced
Achweethie) the river runs in a picturesque "narrow"
known as the Garples, where there is a Garples Pot.

The Chapel path leads to the ruined river church of

Gateway at Fetternear
Church.

Fetternear, which stands beside an ancient walled
kirkyard close to the river. The path branches off to
the left and goes into a field, but your way lies straight
ahead over a short, rough track to where a gate bars
the way. Go through it, turn left, and you are in the
chapel grounds.

Rubble and stones lie all about you and further into
the grounds you come upon the stark remains of what
was obviously a beautiful chapel. Two arched
entrances can still be seen and on the gable is a wall
plaque with the initials IHS and IMJ and a cross above
them.

It is a scene of total desolation. Curious oblong
gravestones lie on the ground, their Latin inscriptions
barely readable. One has the dates 1858–1870. Other
stones lie flat on the ground, including a broken stone
erected by a Peter Walker in memory of his daughter
Isabella, who died in July 1864.

A stone arch with a gate into the cemetery stands a
short distance away. Upright gravestones, erected
surprisingly close together, are almost buried in a

wilderness of ferns and nettles. There is a sad, neglected look about the old kirkyard, almost as if Nature had been closing in on it, hiding it from prying eyes.

The ruined chapel is a comparatively modern building, but it is said that there was a chapel on the site as far back as 1109. St Ninian's Well springs between the church and the river.

Back on the main path, you come upon a short stretch of dyke a short distance beyond the Chapel Pool sign. Two or three steps go up to a narrow path above the track but, whatever its original function, it now leads nowhere, running out among the trees.

On your right, the river ripples on its way, making a great curve to the north as it heads towards Inverurie, Kintore and finally Aberdeen and the sea. There is a saying, "Ae rood o' Don's worth twa o' Dee" (a rood is

a hundred and sixtieth of a Scots acre) and the walk by the river at Fetternear may well persuade you that the old maxim is true. Keep an eye open for swans on the river.

Stick to the right when you come to another fork. A sign, "Lower Hut", indicates a fishing bothy by the river. From here you get your first glimpse of the Shakkin' Briggie.

Shakkin' Briggie.

Continuing on the main path you go through a closed gate (shut it behind you) and in front you will see another entrance to the estate. Beyond it is Whitehaugh Lodge, where there are notices offering honey and bird boxes for sale. The honey is superb! Past the Lodge is a tarred road which turns down towards the river, passing Riverside Cottage. A stone brig crosses a burn running into the Don and the remains of a mill lade can be seen.

Just ahead is a large open space where people going over the bridge can leave their cars. Walkers starting from the Burnhervie side of the estate also park their cars there. It is a long and impressive briggie – and it does shake! You would be well advised to pay attention to the notice, "Do not swing on the bridge".

The road beyond Whitehaugh Lodge runs along a line of beech trees which must have marked a Lovers' Walk at one time – and maybe still does. At any rate, dozens of couples have carved their initials on the trees. One goes back to 1945 and there are probably older ones. It makes you wonder what romantic stories lie behind them. Who were JR and MB, or SB and MK? Will we ever know?

Burnhervie is a quiet little hamlet where roads go off to the Chapel of Garioch, Inverurie and Fetternear and Monymusk. The Don twists and turns on its way to Burnhervie, reminding us of another old saying: "He has as many crooks as the Don". The last pot on this beautiful stretch of river is at Burnhervie – Ree Pot. The word "ree" means a pen for cattle and sheep, and the Ree Pot is the pot beside the enclosure.

Burnhervie is the turning point of the walk, but you have the choice of retracing your steps along the river bank or crossing the Shakkin' Briggie and going back to Kemnay by road. Once over the bridge, there is a steep climb up a path to a lay-by which marks the end of the road.

Whether you arrange for a car to pick you up at the Shakkin' Briggie lay-by or go by foot you set off high above the river, looking down the long sweep of the Don and across to the path that took you to the bridge.

If you are walking, watch out for traffic, for it is a narrow road and there are lots of bends. When you come to a T-junction, turn right, and right again at the next T-junction. You are now in the main road into Kemnay. There is a footpath on the right-hand side of the road, which passes Kemnay Quarry and the Acquithie Road premises of the motor dealers Lawrence of Kemnay. After that, continue until you reach the car park where you left your car.

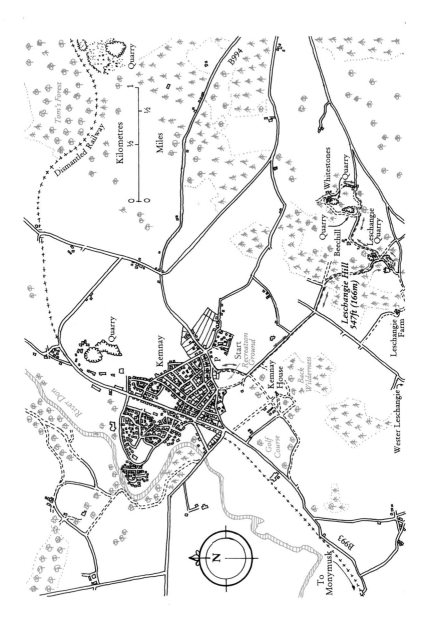

LESCHANGIE HILL

little hill cheated of its chance of fame – that's your destination on this walk from Kemnay. Look for a car park beside the bowling green in Victoria Terrace, the main road into the village. This is your starting point.

At the corner of the bowling green you will see a sign saying "Leschangie". The road to Leschangie is your route, up from the car park and along the edge of Kemnay's recreation ground. At the top of the recreation ground the road bends left. On this minor road traffic is light, but watch out for any cars.

The first tree-lined leg of the walk is through open countryside. Far away on the right you can just pick out the lumpy head of Clachnaben.

Nearer to you, also on your right, Kemnay House is hidden away in a woodland with the curious name of Back Wilderness. The mansion, which dates largely from the 17th century, passed into the hands of the Burnett family in 1688.

Kemnay House has a granite Porter's Lodge which was said to be "the most beautiful lodge in this part of the country". It stands at the entrance to the west avenue, just past the golf course on the Kemnay-Monymusk road. Beautiful though it is, it wasn't built from Kemnay's famous granite – its stone came from the face of Leschangie Hill.

Leschangie Hill lies in front of you as you go up from the car park. You pass a road on the left striking off to North Leschangie and farther uphill the road you are on turns sharp right towards Wester Leschangie.

You part company with it at this corner. As you reach the bend, look for a padlocked gate on the edge of the wood directly in front of you. Go round the side of the gate and follow a stony path until you come to an open area where

INFORMATION

Distance: 6 km (4 miles).

Start and finish: Car park beside bowling green in Victoria Terrace, the main road into Kemnay. Kemnay is 22 km (14 miles) west of Aberdeen.

Terrain: Starts on tarred road, then on woodland track over Leschangie Hill. Strong footwear recommended.

Refreshments: In Kemnay.

Public transport: Bluebird West Gordon Timetable, Service 220 to Kemnay. Information, Tel: (01224 212266).

Main Leschangie quarry.

tracks go to the left and right. In front, two other paths strike into the wood almost side by side. Cross diagonally and take the one on the right – the stony path.

This track goes over Leschangie Hill. It is a comparatively gentle climb – the hill is only 166 m (547 ft) high. As you go down the other side you will see big granite blocks on your left, a reminder of the old quarrying days. A little beyond them a track goes off to the left. You come back this way, but ignore it for the present and carry straight on. Further on you will see another wide track below on your left.

Watch out for a fence on the right. From it, looking down through the trees, you will see what appears to be a pond; it is, in fact, a quarry, the only one that is water-filled.

Just past the quarry the track goes right to Leschangie Farm, but your way is left by the wide, rough track you saw from above. This takes you to a "cross-roads" of tracks. One comes in on the left and goes on downhill to an industrial site, while the track you are on bends a little left and then goes straight ahead through the remains of a gate.

Just beyond the gate on your left is the second quarry. Carry on uphill, taking a look at the panoramic view of the countryside on your right, and you come to a track turning off into the third quarry. This was one of the major quarries, the long arc of its granite face covering a large part of the hill. Two roads run into it and great blocks of pink-grey granite stand on the edge of it. It is bare, bleak and deserted, yet it was from Leschangie Hill that they hacked and blasted granite that was considered to be of a much finer quality than the famous Kemnay granite.

Kemnay granite became known all over the world, pushing Leschangie stone into second place. Yet if Lady Luck had played her cards differently it might have been the other way round. When the Alford Valley Railway was opened, it was decided to take it on an awkward curve round Tom's Forest and past the granite quarries on Paradise Hill to Kemnay.

If another route to the south had been followed it would have passed Leschangie Hill, opening up a rail link from there to the markets. But the trains puffed on to Paradise Hill – and for little Leschangie it was Paradise Lost.

Old road roller at Leschangie.

Follow the track past the quarry until you reach the ruined farm of Beechill. Old farm implements, a cart, a battered and blistered car, cattle feeding troughs and other debris lie scattered about the farm buildings.

From Beechill you go down another track to Whitestones on the east side of Leschangie Hill – and to the last and by far the most impressive quarry. A dusty track leads to the edge of it and you peer cautiously down into the Big Hole – a mini-Rubislaw Quarry.

Whitestones quarry operated throughout the whole of the last century and despite competition from Paradise Hill it quarried stone which went to the building of Waterloo Bridge, London, and the New London Bridge. Some people thought it the best Kemnay granite.

So now you have seen all that remains of the granite glory of Leschangie Hill, the little hill that was always in the shadow of its big sister at Paradise. The walk over the hill and back to Kemnay is pleasant and not too strenuous. When you come to the "cross-roads" on your way back take the track to the right – the short-cut up to the main path. Down at the bottom of the hill you will see the Mither Tap in front of you, marking your way back to the village.

Water-filled quarry.

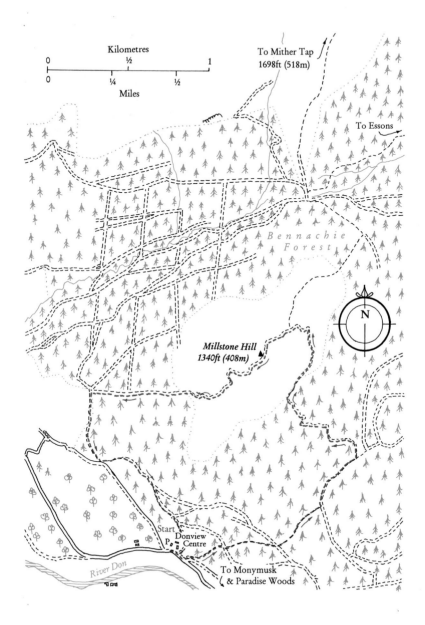

Kilometres

To Mither Tap
1698ft (518m)

To Essons

*Bennachie
Forest*

*Millstone Hill
1340ft (408m)*

N

Start
P Donview
Centre

River Don

To Monymusk
& Paradise Woods

MILLSTONE HILL

Although the Mither Tap draws hundreds of people up the slopes of Bennachie, many walkers prefer to head for its "little sister" – Millstone Hill. Millstone is a spur of Bennachie, rising above the River Don, north of Monymusk, and offering a challenge a little less daunting than the bigger hill. Yet it gives an unsurpassed view of the Garioch countryside and of the Mither Tap itself.

The starting point is the Donview Centre, run by the Forestry Commission. Unfortunately, the centre was closed to the public early in 1995. Outside, there are car parking spaces and picnic tables, toilets, a map of the area, and directions on the routes to take.

Look for posts with red and blue arrows. They can be seen beside the centre and also a little way up the path into the woods. At the start of the walk there is a short tree identification trail. The path climbs up until it meets a broad forest track where red and blue arrowed posts point in two directions.

The red marker, pointing left down the wide track, takes you to the west side of Millstone Hill as part of a short walk from the centre. This walk covers a short stretch of the "red" walk on the last lap of a circular route up and round the hill.

Meantime, however, follow blue arrows up its east side. The first "blue" post is on the opposite side of the forest track, so cross over and continue uphill. It is a steepish climb, but easily tackled if you are reasonably fit.

The Mither Tap is often identified by the lumpy tor on top of it. When you clear the woods look back over your shoulder and you will see another familiar "lump" – the distant peak of Clochnaben.

The path eventually bends to the left and meets another track coming up on the right. Here, the surface, beaten down by bad weather and heavy boots,

INFORMATION

Distance: 5 km (3 miles).

Start and finish: Donview Centre. To get to the Centre take the A96 from Aberdeen, branching off on the B994 to Kemnay. From Kemnay continue to Monymusk on the B993, turning right through the village. Cross the River Don, bearing left, and follow a signposted road to the Donview Centre (the centre is now closed to the public but the car park, toilets and walks are available).

Terrain: Woodland and hill tracks, some rough and narrow. Route down from Millstone Hill is steep and in wet weather can be slippery. Hill boots or strong shoes recommended. Also warm clothing – it can be cold at the top!

Toilets: At Donview Centre.

Refreshments: Nearest shops, cafes, at Monymusk and Kemnay.

Map outside Donview
Centre.

has been fortified by a layer of stones and gravel. There
is a signpost at this fork pointing to Esson's car park
and the Back of Bennachie.

Esson's car park, just off the road from Monymusk to
the Chapel of Garioch, boasts a magnificent new
Bennachie Visitors' Centre. You can see it on the walk
from the Rowan Tree car park (see Walk 23).

Meantime, however, you are on the last lap of the
climb to the rocky summit of Millstone Hill. It is a
hard push, but well worth the effort, for there is no
more impressive view of the Mither Tap than the one
from this outpost of Bennachie.

Standing by the cairn on top of Millstone, Bennachie's
great knotted head provides a breathtaking silhouette
against the sky. It looks huge and formidable against
little Millstone, but the Mither Tap is only 109 m
(358 ft) higher – 408 m (1340 ft) compared with
517 m (1698 ft).

Up there you are looking into Paradise – literally.
Across the Don to the south are Paradise Woods,
planted over two centuries ago by a famous
"improver", Sir Archibald Grant of Monymusk. There
is a narrow pass here called My Lord's Throat, named
after Lord Forbes of Castle Forbes, and when visitors
ask how they could get to Paradise they are told,
"Doon the Lord's Throat".

"Doon the Lord's Throat, an' ootower Bennachie,"
wrote the Garioch poet Charles Murray. Well, we've
been "ootower Bennachie" and now we're heading
down Millstone towards the Lord's Throat. The
descent from the summit is by the official "yellow"
route, but the lower part of it is also covered by green
arrows, which indicate another Bennachie walk from
Donview to the Back of Bennachie. So keep your eyes
open for yellow or yellow/green markers as you
descend.

On your left the grey granite rock of Pitfichie Hill and
Cairn William can be seen rising up behind Paradise
Woods. Millstone Hill takes its name from mill stones

of red granite which were at one time quarried on the hill.

As you go down the hill you can see the Don winding its way through the Garioch towards Monymusk. You can actually pick out the main street of the village. The bridge over the Don at Pitfichie is just discernible without binoculars and to the right of it is Pitfichie Castle.

Not far below the summit you pass an opening where huge rocks rise from the moor and after this you enter woodland. Ahead, you get a lovely glimpse of the distant Don framed in the trees. It is a long, steep climb down a narrow path from the summit. There are lots of stones on the path and tree roots which can be dangerously slippery in wet weather.

Sticking to the yellow markers, you reach another wide forest track where there are both yellow and green markers. They point across the track to other markers where a path continues downhill. There is also a green arrow pointing right along the wide track – ignore it, for this is part of the walk to the Back of Bennachie.

Now into the woods again, you quickly come to a point where you look across lichen-covered dykes into the Don valley. The view stretches across fields and forests to the distant hills. Finally, the path opens up into a wide area where there are two main tracks, one going to the left, the other straight ahead. The track directly ahead leads to the main Donside road near the Centre. The one on the left is part of the "red" route, the short walk, which you saw earlier.

Where the two tracks meet there is a path through the woods to the Donview Centre. This path is marked at the junction by both red and yellow markers.

At the end of your walk you will be a "convert" to Bennachie's "sister" hill.

Mither Tap from path to Millstone Hill.

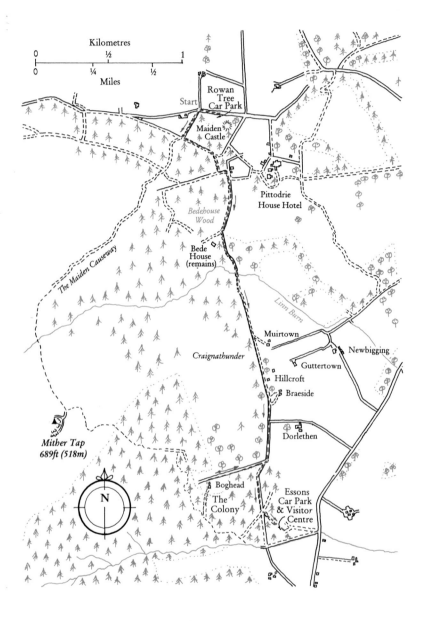

Kilometres

Miles

Rowan
Tree
Car Park

Start

Maiden
Castle

Pittodrie
House Hotel

*Bedehouse
Wood*

Bede
House
(remains)

The Maiden Causeway

Lim Burn

Muirtown

Newbigging

Guttertown

Craignathunder

Hillcroft

Braeside

Dorlethen

*Mither Tap
689ft (518m)*

Boghead

The
Colony

Essons
Car Park
& Visitor
Centre

N

UNDER THE MITHER TAP

Although hundreds of people climb Bennachie from the Rowan Tree car park, it is unlikely that many of them notice a narrow path cutting away to the left near the foot of the hill. The path links Bennachie's two main car parks – the Rowan Tree and Esson's car park – and for those who want a pleasant low-level walk away from the windy heights of the Mither Tap it is ideal.

What's more, there are interesting things to see at the end of the walk – firstly, the magnificent new Bennachie Visitors' Centre, where you can learn all about the lore and legend of the area, and secondly, the Colony.

The Rowan Tree car park is attractively laid out, with toilets, picnic tables above the parking area, a map of Bennachie and its seven peaks, and an information board about the Mither Tap. The Maiden Causeway runs from the car park to the summit. Its origins are unknown, although one fanciful tale says that a local laird imprisoned and raped maidens in the fort on the top of the hill. On the other hand, some maps show a Maiden Castle at the foot of the hill.

The path to Esson's is less than 400 m up the Maiden's Causeway. Look for it on the left when you come to an open grassy area. In summer it is sometimes obscured by undergrowth. It runs along the edge of the forest – on the left there is a panoramic view of the Garioch countryside – and then it slips into the woods.

The path widens a little as you move on and where it swings downhill to the left it becomes a double track. As it turns to the right the rooftops of a cottage can be seen. Round the corner is a back entrance to Pittodrie House Hotel. Just inside the entrance gate is a path to the cottage you saw – the Pittodrie kennels.

Passing the gate, you keep going straight ahead. If you look back on your left you can see Pittodrie House Hotel nestling in the trees. It is an interesting building, dating back to the early 17th century.

INFORMATION

Distance: 6.5 km (4 miles).

Start and finish: Rowan Tree car park. To get there take the A96 Aberdeen-Inverness road, branching off beyond Inverurie on the road to Chapel of Garioch. Continue through Chapel of Garioch until you come to a sign pointing left on the road to the Rowan Tree car park.

Terrain: Path narrow at first, but widens later. Reasonable walking. Strong footwear recommended.

Toilets: Rowan Tree car park and at Esson's car park.

Worth seeing: Bennachie Visitor Centre and the Colony.

Transport: Car necessary.

Opening Hours: *Bennachie Centre:* Apr.-Oct., weekends 1000–1700, summer weeks 1200–1600 (likely to be closed on Mondays); Nov.-Mar., weekends 1100–1530, weekdays (Thurs. & Fri.) 1200–1500, closed Mon., Tues., Wed., these times are subject to change.

The wood on the right is known as Bedehouse Wood, and somewhere among the trees are the remains of a Bede House (almshouse). It stood by the Linn Burn near Pittodrie House and there is an interesting tale attached to it. In the time of King Charles II it was built by William Erskine of Pittodrie for four poor men. It consisted of "two chambers and one mid-room". The four men were each given one peck of meal and half a peck of malt each week, but they had to wear livery gowns and go to church on Sundays.

Beautiful old birch trees can be seen on the right as you head along the track, which goes downhill and then climbs again. When you come to a fork keep left. Across the fields the farm of Newbigging can be seen. At this point – about halfway between the Rowan Tree car park and Esson's – a craig on Bennachie, which rises on your right, is shown on maps as Craignathunder, pronounced Craignathunner.

This has been dismissed as a distortion of an old name, but James Macdonald, a well-known place-name expert a century ago, thought that "thunder" was a fragment of a Gaelic hill-name, *Ton re gaoith*, meaning "backside to the wind". Whether or not you have your backside to the wind on the walk to Esson's doesn't really matter – you're nicely sheltered by the trees below the thundering craig!

Watch out for a wooden gate on your left. In the fields below it three houses can be seen. The two nearest are painted white, the second with a conservatory at the gable-end. The first is Muirton and the second Guttertown, while farther on is Newbigging. Beyond that the fields stretch away to the horizon.

Farther on is Hill Croft and Braeside, while beyond that a road goes down to the farm of Dorlethen. There is a sinister story about Dorlethen. In a letter

Bennachie.

written in 1938, George Esson, who was a crofter on Bennachie for nearly 50 years, mentioned the death of the Dorlethen farmer, a man called Hay.

On the Rowan Tree walk.

"There was a very mysterious occurrence about a child of his step-daughter," he wrote. "It was lost. It disappeared away from Dorlethen and its body was found on the Hill when they were cutting trees 7 years afterwards at the head of the Boddach road. It was just 22 months old and it could not manage to climb up there by itself, I don't think. There was a Public Enquiry in Aberdeen but nothing was decided about it as there was no evidence."

Dorlethen looks innocent enough today. After you pass it the path narrows again as you go through the woods to Esson's car park. When you come to a fork you can see the new Bennachie Centre at the end of the left-hand track.

From the Centre it is worthwhile extending your walk to take in the Colony. The Colony began with a handful of squatters, but by 1859 there were nearly 60 crofters living in 12 homesteads on the hill. They were harried by local lairds who wanted to divide the hill between themselves. One by one they left the area until finally only one remained – John Esson, whose son George lived there until 1939. Hence the name Esson's car park.

The Colony lay buried in the woods for more than half a century, but in 1993 work began on clearing the area and "unveiling" the old crofts. They had names like Cunningstone, Hillside, and Boghead (Esson's croft).

It is a little bit of Bennachie history and well worth seeing. From the Colony return to the Centre and make your way back from Esson's to the Rowan Tree car park.

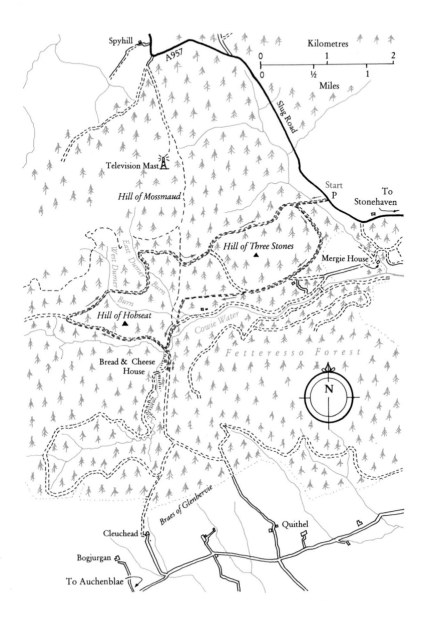

CRYNE'S CROSS MOUNTH

The ancient Grampian pass known as the Cryne's Corse (or Cross) Mounth was said to run from "ye church of S. Paladius vulgarly called pade kirke in ye Mearns to ye Mylles of Drum" on Deeside. Today, most of it is lost in the heather, but this walk takes you down one side of the pass and up the other. It also covers sections that are still traceable and others still in use.

Coming from Drum, the original route went from the farm of Spyhill on the Slug Road over the Hill of Mossmaud to the ITV television mast, then down into Fetteresso Forest. Your starting point is 3 km south-east of Spyhill (see Information), where a car park has been laid out by the Forestry Commission at the start of a new mountain bike trail.

The trail, which can also be used by walkers, starts near an Information Board with a map of the Fetteresso and Drumtochty woodlands. It climbs uphill to a green marker post, where it does a kind of U-turn and goes left in the direction indicated by a yellow arrow. Ignore a track going directly ahead – that's on the return route.

Farther on you come to another marker post with a yellow arrow again pointing straight ahead. A track going downhill on the left leads to a road through the forest from Mergie House, just off the Slug Road, but that is not your route.

As you head west through Fetteresso, still following the yellow marker, you go round the lower slopes of

INFORMATION

Distance: 9.5 km (6 miles).

Start and finish: Car park at start of marked mountain bike trail on the Slug Road (A97), which runs from the South Deeside Road (A943) to Stonehaven. Follow the Slug Road, passing Spyhill (look for sign on right) after 5 km. About 3 km further on, look for an opening on the right with a Mountain Bike Trail signpost. Car park is a little way up the track.

Terrain: Mountain bike track, then woodland track, rough in parts. Good walking shoes or hill boots recommended.

Refreshments: Small cafe on Slug Road at Cairn-mon-earn, otherwise at Banchory or Stonehaven.

Transport: Car necessary.

Track in Fetteresso Forest.

the Hill of Three Stones. Interestingly, there is a Hill of the Nine Stanes west of Spyhill. The countryside opens up as you walk. On the left you look down on the Cowie Water, catching glimpses of the Mergie road. Then another junction looms up, with a track going uphill to the right. Pass it and move on.

As you head along the track it begins to drop down to the Cowie Water. Watch out for a burn tumbling down from the hill on your right. This is the East Dumer Burn. The East and West Dumer Burns gives a more accurate idea of where the Cryne's Cross pass lay. It is unlikely that it followed an undeviating line, but this was roughly the way it came. Near here, on the north side of the Cowie, there was an inn for travellers going over the Mounth, and a little way on is another link with the past.

To reach it, go right when your track meets the Mergie road at the Cowie Water. A short distance away is another marker post. The familiar yellow arrow points ahead, while a red arrow points to a track cutting away to the left. Go left, crossing an open-sided bridge over the Cowie.

It may have been here that Rabbie Burns first thought of a cryptic piece of verse that he later put on paper. He composed it, not because he thought it a lovely spot (which it is), but because he wanted to cock a snook at the Laird of Mergie. The stane Hoose o' Mergie dates back to the 17th century and the Bard had a fleeting association with it when he poached the Cowie Water. Caught in the act, he threw his rod away and made his escape. Later, with typical contempt for the gentry, he penned the lines:

> Your fish are scarce, your water's sma',
> There's my rod – and Rab's awa'!

Burns probably hot-footed it away from the Cowie on one of the tracks of your walk, for to the north are the Braes of Glenbervie, where his relatives lived. Not far from the river the road forks. The track on the right goes to Cleuchead, near the farm of Bogjurgan, where William Burnes, Burns' great grand-uncle farmed, while not far away is Brawliemuir, where his grandfather, Robert Burnes, was born and brought up.

The track on the left ends up at Quithel, near the Stonehaven-Auchenblae road, where there is a Forestry Commission car park.

Bread and Cheese House (ruin).

When Rabbie Burns wasn't poaching the Laird of Mergie's fish, he may have idled away an hour or two at the inn on the north side of the Cowie or at a "Bread and Cheese" house known as Lady's Leys, near the Cleuchead-Quithel fork. The name Lady's Leys was probably a corruption of Ladylea, which comes from the Gaelic *leathad liath*, meaning a grey slope.

The old "Bread and Cheese" house is still there, or at least what is left of it. Look for it on the bank on your right – the grey slope – when you go up the brae. Its ruined walls suggest a solid and substantial building, no doubt used by drovers going over Cryne's Cross Mounth on their way to the great cattle market on Herscha Hill, near Auchenblae. It was known as Paldy Fair, after St Palladius, who gave his name to the "pade kirk".

Here, however, you leave Lady's Leys and the drovers and retrace your steps, going down over the Cowie bridge and turning left. The track wanders along the edge of the Hill of Hobseat, with pleasant views on your left, and finally comes to a clearing or turning-point where another track goes off to the right.

This is your way back. The track crosses the East Dumer Burn and you will see the ITV mast beckoning you in the distance. When you come to another open area where the road splits in two go left, following one more yellow marker until power pylons and hills can be seen in front of you.

Soon you are passing your first marker post and going downhill to the Information Board and the car park.

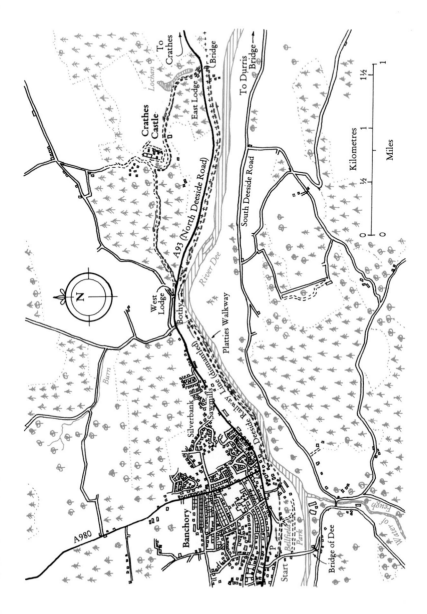

BANCHORY TO CRATHES

"A pearl of great price among the nation's jewels" – that's how Crathes Castle was once described by the historian Dr W. Douglas Simpson. This walk takes you to Crathes by the old Deeside railway line, where one of the lairds of Crathes had his own personal Halt when the trains were running.

From the Dee Street car park in Banchory, take a tarmac path going east through Bellfield Park, with the North Deeside Road (A93) on your left and the River Dee on your right. After passing under an old railway bridge, go right by a footpath which skirts a housing estate built on the site of Banchory railway station.

This takes you to a steep embankment above the Dee, where you will see steps going down to the river. A notice tells you that they lead to the Platties Walkway, which runs along the edge of the water. Ignore the walkway at this point – you'll see it on your way back.

Instead, continue along the path until you come to the old engine sheds. The station was built on the site of the original village of Banchory. It was the terminus of the Deeside Railway, but there is little left to remind you of that glorious era.

One Deeside author, James Coutts, didn't think much of the station. In his Dictionary of Deeside in 1899 he said it was "a station which is neither well built nor well situated, being placed at the eastern outskirts

INFORMATION

Distance: 9.5 km (6 miles).

Start and finish: Dee Street car park, Banchory. Banchory is 30 km (18 miles) west of Aberdeen on A93.

Terrain: Paths in park, then old railway track to Crathes Castle. Take care if including Platties Walkway on the return journey.

Toilets: In Banchory and at Crathes Castle.

Refreshments: Cafe at Crathes, also an abundance of eating places in Banchory.

Public transport: Good bus service from Aberdeen to Banchory and Crathes.

Public Transport: Bluebird Coach Timetable, Service 201. Information: (01224 212266).

Opening Hours: *Crathes Castle:* 1 Apr.- 23 Oct., 1100–1730 daily. Last admission 1645. Admission charge: Garden and grounds open all year daily, 0930-sunset.

River Dee near Crathes.

Mort-house in Banchory-
Ternan kirkyard.

close to the churchyard, as if designed for nearness to the dead rather than the living".

The gateway into the kirkyard is on your left and when you go through it you will see a building that was erected when other people were showing a gruesome interest in the dead. This is an unusual two-storeyed circular mort-house used as a Watch Tower when body-snatchers were on the prowl. It has a bell made by Peter Ostens of Rotterdam in 1644.

Take the wide track to the left of the Watch Tower and when you come to the end of a low wall on your right, turn right and rejoin the track.

Here you will see another sign at the end of the Platties Walkway, but don't go down to it unless you want to cut your walk short and return to Bellfield Park. Instead, bear left and go back on to the railway line.

The Silverbank Sawmills are on your left and on the right you come to an open space where anglers are usually seen. A track goes up to the sawmill and the railway track does a small twist and continues on its way, but look for another path going into the woods directly in front of you. It runs parallel with the main track, but it is closer to the river and gives you pleasant views of the Dee.

Further on, a bridge spans a burn running into the Dee and some rough steps take you up the embankment to the railway line. Beyond the bridge another path takes you back to the riverbank. There are stepping stones over the burn, but when the stream is swollen by rain this is not advised.

Soon you will see a fishing bothy ahead; this is where you turn up to the old railway line. Go through a gate, past the bothy and up the embankment, through another small gate, and on to the main track. On the other side of the line a small path continues up to what was a stretch of the North Deeside Road and is now a lay-by. Near here on the present A93 is the West Gate of Crathes Castle. Your destination, however, is the East

Gate of the castle, so keep heading along the old line, which runs close to the main road.

The bridge at Durris and the masts on Cairn mon Earn can be seen in the distance. Across the road on your left, behind a dyke, a big sign says "Crathes Castle and Gardens". A little way ahead is another sign and beside it an opening where you can get out on to the North Deeside Road, but if you want to avoid the traffic stick to the railway track a little longer.

Keep an eye open for St Ternan's football field on the right – it is directly opposite the entrance to Crathes Castle. The track dips down and goes under a bridge on the A93, taking you on to the main avenue into the estate.

Crathes Castle.

The walk up the avenue, passing a lovely lochan on the right, will take you to the castle, one of the finest in the north-east, and now in the care of the National Trust for Scotland.

Your way back is by the West Gate. Look for a tarmac road going past the castle. Ignore paths going left or right – stick to the main route to the West Gate, passing Caroline's Garden.

When you reach the West Gate turn left on to the North Deeside Road, cross the road to the other side and watch for a path going down into the old road lay-by. From here another path takes you on to the Deeside line. Follow the railway track until you come to the path which takes you down to the riverbank and Platties Walkway.

The Platties takes its name from the concrete platforms used in the building of it. Early this century, when the station underwent substantial rebuilding, the project included the construction alongside the River Dee of a massive retaining wall with a right of way at its foot known as the Platties.

There is a fine view up the river, where the Feugh comes tumbling into join it, and in the distance you can see the familiar tower on Scolty Hill. From the Platties it is an easy walk back to Bellfield Park and your car.

INDEX

Other titles in this series

25 Walks – Deeside
25 Walks – Dumfries and Galloway
25 Walks – Edinburgh and Lothian
25 Walks – Fife
25 Walks – In and Around Glasgow
25 Walks – Highland Perthshire
25 Walks – The Trossachs

Other titles in preparation

25 Walks – The Scottish Borders

Long distance guides published by HMSO

The West Highland Way – Official Guide
The Southern Upland Way – Official Guide

HMSO Bookshops
71 Lothian Road, Edinburgh EH3 9AZ
0131-228 4181 Fax 0131-229 2734
49 High Holborn, London WC1V 6HB
(counter service only)
0171-873 0011 Fax 0171-831 1326
68–69 Bull Street, Birmingham B4 6AD
0121-236 9696 Fax 0121-236 9699
33 Wine Street, Bristol BS1 2BQ
0117 9264306 Fax 0117 9294515
9-21 Princess Street, Manchester M60 8AS
0161-834 7201 Fax 0161-833 0634
16 Arthur Street, Belfast BT1 4GD
01232 238451 Fax 01232 235401
The HMSO Oriel Bookshop, The Friary, Cardiff CF1 4AA
01222 395548 Fax 01222 384347

HMSO publications are available from:

HMSO Publications Centre
(Mail, fax and telephone orders only)
PO Box 276, London SW8 5DT
Telephone orders 0171-873 9090
General enquiries 0171-873 0011
(queuing system in operation for both numbers)
Fax orders 0171-873 8200

HMSO's Accredited Agents
(see Yellow Pages)

and through good booksellers